Breaking the Power of Shame
FREEDOM

Ralph Ennis, Judy Gomoll, Rebecca Goldstone, Dennis Stokes, and Christine Weddle

D1529987

NavPress is the publishing ministry of The Navigators, an international Christian organization and leader in personal spiritual development. NavPress is committed to helping people grow spiritually and enjoy lives of meaning and hope through personal and group resources that are biblically rooted, culturally relevant, and highly practical.

**For a free catalog go to www.NavPress.com
or call 1.800.366.7788 in the United States or 1.800.839.4769 in Canada.**

© 2010 by The Navigators

All rights reserved. No part of this publication may be reproduced in any form without written permission from NavPress, P.O. Box 35001, Colorado Springs, CO 80935. www.navpress.com

NAVPRESS and the NAVPRESS logo are registered trademarks of NavPress. Absence of ® in connection with marks of NavPress or other parties does not indicate an absence of registration of those marks.

ISBN-13: 978-1-60006-666-5

Cover Design by The DesignWorks Group, Jason Gabbert, www.thedesignworksgroup.com
Royalty-free images provided by: Photos.com, IStock.com, stockxchng.com, Dreamstime.com, Crestock photos, and Bigstockphotos.com
Contributors: Ralph Ennis, Judy Gomoll, Rebecca Goldstone, Dennis Stokes, and Christine Weddle

Some of the anecdotal illustrations in this book are true to life and are included with the permission of the persons involved. All other illustrations are composites of real situations, and any resemblance to people living or dead is coincidental.

Unless otherwise identified, all Scripture quotations in this publication are taken from the *HOLY BIBLE: NEW INTERNATIONAL VERSION*® (NIV®). Copyright © 1973, 1978, 1984 by International Bible Society. Used by permission of Zondervan Publishing House. All rights reserved. Other versions used include: *THE MESSAGE* (MSG). Copyright © 1993, 1994, 1995, 1996, 2000, 2001, 2002, 2005. Used by permission of NavPress Publishing Group; the *Holy Bible, New Living Translation* (NLT), copyright © 1996, 2004. Used by permission of Tyndale House Publishers, Inc., Carol Stream, Illinois 60188. All rights reserved; the *Amplified Bible* (AMP), © The Lockman Foundation 1954, 1958, 1962, 1964, 1965, 1987; *The Holy Bible, New Century Version*, copyright © 1987, 1988, 1991 by Word Publishing, Dallas, Texas 75039. Used by permission; the *New American Standard Bible* (NASB), © The Lockman Foundation 1960, 1962, 1963, 1968, 1971, 1972, 1973, 1975, 1977, 1995; the *Revised Standard Version Bible* (RSV), copyright 1946, 1952, 1971, by the Division of Christian Education of the National Council of the Churches of Christ in the USA. Used by permission, all rights reserved; *The Living Bible* (TLB). Copyright © 1971. Used by permission of Tyndale House Publishers, Inc., Wheaton, IL 60189, all rights reserved; and the Holy Bible, *Today's New International*® *Version* (TNIV)®. Copyright © 2001, 2005 by International Bible Society®. Used by permission of International Bible Society. All rights reserved worldwide.

Printed in China

1 2 3 4 5 6 7 8 / 12 11 10

CONTENTS

INTRODUCTION
BEFORE YOU SELECT THIS STUDY

. . . SOMETHING TO THINK ABOUT!

There's something for almost everyone in this study. That's because almost everybody has struggled with shame over *something* — pimples or porn, aging or abuse, a report card or a terrible family secret. We also long to experience freedom from the smog and destruction of shame on our souls. This study will point you in the direction of mercy and hope for your journey.

But this study may not be for everybody. That's because the core topics (guilt, shame, and transforming change) are personal and can be risky and painful depending on one's background and past experiences. Honor the reality that not every person, small group, or mentoring relationship is ready to go there. Just a heads-up.

So before you launch into this study, we recommend two prerequisites:

- **Have several months of experience together** as a small group or mentoring relationship before going through this study, perhaps doing another book in the Connect series. This experience will allow your group to create a safe, grace-filled environment and build trust before tackling the topic of shame.
- **Devote your first session** to discussing chapter 1. This introductory chapter will get you off to a good start and won't require any advance preparation for group members. It will also draw out where members are in their thinking and feelings about shame.

SOME COMMON QUESTIONS WHEN DISCUSSING SHAME

WHAT MAKES DISCUSSING "SHAME" DIFFERENT FROM OTHER TOPICS OR STUDIES?

Typical Bible study discussions often focus on facts, knowledge, principles, truths—with some application and heart questions, too. While relevant and helpful, they are usually emotionally neutral. But discussing shame touches soul and identity-level issues that include emotional pain and often trigger deep feelings. This may be new territory for a group more used to topics like prayer or faith. The good news is that bringing these issues into the light of trusted community with the hope of Scripture can propel our spiritual journeys toward wholeness in Christ.

WHY CAN'T I JUST FIX MY SHAME ISSUES ON MY OWN?

Shame keeps things hidden in the dark. When trying harder on our own to solve issues doesn't work, what's missing is often true community. God often uses others to channel His healing grace, life-giving truth, and abundant kindness into our lives. Maybe in the past you've been afraid of being alone in the discussion or you risked and got burned by someone's judgment or rejection. As a group, you can create trusted, confidential community for sharing acceptance and connection. You can validate each other's pain without minimizing it. Invite others to move from isolation toward authentic friendships that can bear the weight of truth—even truth we're ashamed of exposing.

DO I REALLY HAVE TO TELL MY STORY?

As you walk alongside someone struggling with shame, you can help by being transparent about your own struggles—past or present. Personal example can powerfully speak safety and hope. Our vulnerability can give permission for others to respond with love, acceptance, and guidance. You don't have to explain all the details, but share enough to be real and illustrate being broken. When our stories involve confessing the stark truth about our shame, the first response from others needs to be compassionate. That means acknowledging the struggle, accepting the person (not any sinful behavior attached to it), and offering mercy and hope.

WHAT COMMON REACTIONS COULD SHUT SOMEONE DOWN?

- **Spiritualizing:** Like saying, "There must be sin in your life" or "You just need to pray more."
- **Comparing Stories:** Like saying, "I know just how you feel . . ." and then launching into your own story. Or saying, "Hey, that's nothing compared to . . . it could have turned out so much worse."
- **Minimizing:** Like saying "It's not that bad" or "Just think about the positive" or excusing or making less of another's experience.
- **Being embarrassed:** For example, when you feel uncomfortable or ashamed, rolling your eyes, laughing inappropriately, or withdrawing emotionally or physically from the person sharing.

WHAT IF SOMETHING FEELS TOO DIFFICULT FOR OUR GROUP TO ADDRESS OR WE NEED HOPE?

Consider professional help if you see signs of someone spiraling down into depression, self-destructive behaviors, or suicidal tendencies. Have a list of local professional resources available. So relax! Remember that the Holy Spirit is the true leader of your group—and your Counselor, Healer, Comforter, Truth-teller, and Encourager. You don't need to give each other advice, have all the answers, or be a therapist. Creating space to just be heard is healing in itself. One of shame's most persistent lies is to whisper into our struggling hearts, "Nobody else struggles with this. This is who you *are!* And nothing will ever change!" There is no sin or shame you can imagine that is stronger than God's love! *There is hope* for the victims and the abusers among us, and for all of us whose own sinful choices make them ashamed. As a group, point each other to God's promises, mercy and kindness He's the only One who can cover and wash away shame for good.

GUIDELINES FOR SMALL GROUPS

It is the facilitator's or leader's responsibility to help the group members follow these guidelines for the protection of all as you build trust. So read these guidelines together.

1. **Confidentiality:** Don't repeat anything said inside the group to anyone outside the group.

2. **Safety:** Respect each other's boundaries. Also accept each others' perceived realities without needing to comment or "fix" how they feel or see things at the moment. Nobody should feel forced to share anything that they prefer to keep private.

3. **"I" Statements:** Be yourself; be willing to start taking off your masks. Share only about yourself — not others.

4. **Interference:** Avoid giving advice, talking while someone else is sharing, or subtle competition by saying "I'm just like you" or by sharing a similar story. Instead, listen, learn, and affirm.

5. **Individuality:** Accept and enjoy the diversity in your group, including being at very different places on your spiritual journeys. Avoid probing or intrusive questioning as well as elaborating on each other's personal sharing.

6. **Emotional Sharing:** Allow each other to experience a full range of emotion, including crying, raising their voice, or being silent. When this happens (even if it makes you uncomfortable), avoid words or body language that will shut someone down. Also avoid touching or hugging without permission. Allow for times of quiet in your group, because silence can be one of the most powerful environments for healing and spiritual transformation.

7. **Roadblocks and Obstacles:** Let people process their thoughts and feelings without needing to come to clear resolution. Being stuck can be a catalyst to move forward or for further reflection. Trust God to use the process! It's okay to leave some questions hanging.

8. **Holy Spirit:** Recognize that true life-change only occurs with God's help as we yield to His leading. The group can provide a place for God's love to be modeled and felt, and where God's truth can be discovered and trusted. It might also provide accountability through prayer and support on your journeys of spiritual formation and transformation.

9. **Group Limits:** Don't expect your group to be qualified to provide therapy, counseling, or other in-depth one-to-one support for members. Know when to refer each other to someone outside your group who is better equipped to help.

10. **Pace:** Some groups study a whole chapter each week. They prepare all of the questions but only discuss selected ones. Other groups devote two weeks to each chapter. Find a pace that allows you to truly meet with God — not just finish an academic exercise.

From these guidelines, what do you especially want the others in your group to remember so that you can feel safe to be transparent?

Which of these guidelines might you tend to forget about?

CHAPTER FLOW

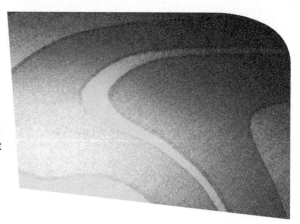

Think of your time spent in each chapter as a journey . . . an exploratory trip toward authentic spiritual transformation. Most chapters in this study have the following sections where you will "pause" your heart and mind along the way.

A SHORT STORY

Each chapter begins with a person's story based on real-life experiences.

PAUSE 1

This first section invites you into the story of some real people in the Bible who struggled with shame. Try placing yourself in these stories as you imagine the dynamics and emotions going on.

PAUSES 2 AND 3

Each chapter will have two more pauses where you will consider what God says in His Word about this topic of shame. In these sections you will:

- Begin to identify where you are in terms of shame and how you got there
- Explore biblical principles for breaking the power of shame in your life
- Find helpful background information about shame (its emotions, sources, hiding styles)

PAUSE 4

We just aren't strong enough by ourselves to resist the messages of accusation and condemnation that trigger our shame. So this closing section called "Breaking the Power of Shame" and "Voices of Mercy" invites God to speak words of mercy and hope into your hearts through your group members. It also provides a list of key ideas from the chapter.

SCRIPTURE MEMORY

We strongly encourage you to meditate on and memorize the key verse suggested for each chapter as a way of building this vital spiritual habit into your journey. See pages 149-151 for practical suggestions on memorizing Scripture and a list of all the suggested memory verses.

IMAGES

In each chapter we've included pictures and artwork to help you reflect on the topics. They are there to stimulate your imagination and heart. Take time to gaze at the images and place yourself within these visual stories. If a photo disturbs you, that's okay; try to figure out why.

YOUR JOURNEY THROUGH EACH CHAPTER

For each chapter, expect to devote about an hour or more to personal preparation — so pace yourself. You might try:

- working a little at a time on a chapter
- using your devotional or quiet time to process the study during the week
- doing the whole study in one focused sitting

After a few chapters you'll find a rhythm that fits you. Your group may decide whether to discuss a whole chapter at one sitting or just a part of each chapter.

GETTING YOU STARTED

To get the most from your study, we encourage you to do five simple things:

1. Read the verses meditatively, inviting the Holy Spirit to help you unpack what He wants you to understand from each verse. We've printed out many of the Bible passages for you from a variety of Bible translations, mostly from the *New International Version* (NIV). Sometimes we quote from other translations for a fresh rendering, such as *The Message* (MSG), *The New Living Translation* (NLT), etc. And you'll need to look up some passages in your own Bible.
2. Mark the verses to help you engage as you read. Be creative! Underline, draw circles or arrows ———▶, highlight, use colored pencils — whatever will help you process as you go.
3. Be aware of your own responses and emotions. This study is about a core human experience: shame. As you authentically embrace your internal world, let the Spirit of God use the Scriptures and others to speak deeply into your heart.
4. Write or draw something for each question. This study is meant to feel like a journal — not a workbook. Some of you may fill up every square inch of white space with writing. But even if you're not into journaling, try to write something — even a few words or a scribble — in response to every question.
5. Pray throughout your study. Ask God to shed light on what you're studying and to help you connect what you read to the realities in your life.

CHAPTER 1
SHAME AT FIRST GLANCE

It was the Fourth of July. Three families parked in the lot next to a church and spread out their blankets and chairs to watch the fireworks. Before long nine-year-old Ryan was fidgety. "Ryan, how many times do I have to tell you to sit down and shut up? Can't you do anything right?" his mother scolded.

To kill time before the show, Ryan's dad told the other families about their recent vacation trip. "Riding in the car with Ryan is such a pain. I mean — he stinks! The kid passes so much gas that we practically had to stop every five miles to air out the car." Everyone laughed as Ryan blushed in shame and stared at his tennis shoes. "I think we'll just tie him down in the back of the pick-up next summer — so we can all breathe!"

Humiliated, Ryan pinched his little sister. "Ryan!" yelled his dad. "For the hundredth time, try acting your age. You ought to be ashamed of yourself! — and right here by the church!"

What do you think words like these did to Ryan's heart?

How have you seen children shamed by adults?

Is there anything in Ryan's story that you can identify with? If so, explain.

PAUƎ 1_HOW IT ALL
ƎTARTED

It's the age-old story of humanity's fall:

> *GENESIS 3:8-10. Then the man and his wife heard the sound of the Lᴏʀᴅ God as he was walking in the garden in the cool of the day, and they hid from the Lᴏʀᴅ God among the trees of the garden. But the Lᴏʀᴅ God called to the man, "Where are you?"*
>
> *He answered, "I heard you in the garden, and I was afraid because I was naked; so I hid."*

Adam and Eve experienced **guilt**. Guilt probably said to them:

> *You've disobeyed God.*
> *You've done something wrong.*
> *You broke the only rule He gave you.*

They also felt **ashamed**. Maybe Shame said to them:

> *You are not what you used to be.*
> *You are not good.*
> *You are bad.*
> *You are worthless.*
> *You are powerless to change.*
> *You deserve to be punished.*
> *You don't deserve to be loved.*

Maybe they thought, "The problem isn't just *what I've done*. The problem is rooted in *who I am*."

GUILT:
My inner critical voice saying, "I have done something wrong." A sense of violating a standard.

SHAME:
My inner critical voice saying, "I am flawed." A sense of being deeply defective or unworthy.

Sᴏ Aᴅᴀᴍ ᴀɴᴅ Eᴠᴇ ʜɪᴅ.

Aɴᴅ Sɪɴ ʜᴀᴅ ɪᴛꜱ ꜰɪʀꜱᴛ ᴄᴀꜱᴜᴀʟᴛɪᴇꜱ.

HOW WOULD YOU DESCRIBE SHAME?

To feel the sting of something that humiliates you is to be dipped into the experience of shame — the most toxic of all emotions. . . . Somehow you feel exposed. Weighed in the balance and found wanting. Humiliated. It's such a miserable experience that generally, we avoid it at all costs.

— Paula Rinehart,
Better Than My Dreams

We may trust God with our past as heartily as with our future. It will not hurt so long as we do not try to hide things, so long as we are ready to bow our heads in hearty shame where it is fit that we should be ashamed. For to be ashamed is a holy and blessed thing.

Shame is a thing to shame only those who want to appear, not those who want to be. Shame is to shame those who want to pass their examination, not those who want to get into the heart of things. . . . To be humbly ashamed is to be plunged in the cleansing bath of truth.

— From *An Anthology of George MacDonald*,
Edited by C. S. Lewis

SO WHICH IS IT?! IS SHAME:

humiliating and miserable . . . or . . . holy, blessed, and cleansing?

THE WORLD OF SHAME IS CONFUSING AND COMPLEX.

BUT WE WILL FIND HOPE ON OUR JOURNEY TO FREEDOM!

PAUSE 2_
EXPLORING SHAME — WHY IT'S IMPORTANT

Why study shame? You may be thinking, *Why an entire Bible study on the topic of shame? Sounds depressing. Can't we just take our sins to the cross, read Scripture, and experience Jesus' forgiveness?* If that's how you feel, this study will expose you to the complexity of the topic. And it will prepare you to come alongside your friends and family experiencing the deep wounds of shame with sensitivity and compassion.

Why not avoid shame? Or you may be thinking, *Talk about shame?! I'd rather get my leg amputated without anesthesia! The experience of shame has been so painful that there's no way I want to stir up all those feelings and memories I've tried so hard to bury.* If that sounds like you, this study will help you connect with biblical characters who felt much like you have. And it will provide an atmosphere of grace to explore your shame with trusted others in your group — maybe for the first time. Our prayer is that you'll find Jesus seeking you out in your shame so you can receive His mercy, healing, and new freedom.

Shame is universal. Our first awareness of sin may come through guilt — and certainly all of us are, in fact, guilty of falling short of God's standards. Some of us also have serious things we're ashamed of — sinful addictions or devastating abuse. Most of us grapple with "smaller" stuff — the shame of unpleasant body issues, not making the team, not getting the promotion, or losing your temper *again* — but whatever its "size," we all experience shame in varying degrees and situations. We go out of our way to avoid it. It is amazing how much of our behavior stems from an unrecognized need to *avoid shame, cover shame,* or *deny shame.*

What types of shame are there? Sometimes shame happens when we've really blown it and deserve to be ashamed. That comes with being part of the sin-prone human race. It is intended to usher us into God's healing presence, into the bath of His forgiveness, into His loving mercy. At other times shame is heaped on us over things we aren't responsible for and don't deserve. It can drive people into utter darkness, desolation, and separation from life.

Is this a dangerous study? So there's shame that alerts us . . . and then there's shame that just hurts us. If you've suffered deep abuse or pain of any kind, discussing this subject may trigger inner screams of accusation, "It's all my fault! I deserve the condemnation and pain." If this triggers despair, we urge you to seek appropriate professional support.

Where is God in all this? For others who have shame grouped with other "bad emotions," this study will open your eyes to why God designed us with the capacity to feel shame — and to Satan's skill in twisting shame into something lethal. As we honestly face our shame, we'll be drawn to Jesus — the only lasting solution to our shame.

Our prayer. We, the authors, are in our own process of healing and spiritual transformation. We're continually facing our shame, tasting the acceptance and mercy of God and other people, tuning out voices of condemnation and tuning in voices of mercy and truth. We're finding freedom, intimacy, and mercy in Jesus. That's our hope and prayer for you, the reader.

What would your group like to gain from studying this topic together?

Maybe right now you can't really identify with feelings of shame. Maybe it will help to think of shame as one of a whole family of emotions. As you read through this list, highlight several feelings that you connect with being ashamed. Explain.

Alienated	Embarrassed	Inferior	Shy
Belittled	Exposed	Insecure	Stigmatized
Defeated	Flawed	Intimidated	Unlovable
Degraded	Helpless	Invisible	Unworthy
Defenseless	Humiliated	Odd	Weak
Different	Hurt	Powerless	Worthless
Dumped	Inadequate	Rejected	

What if . . . ? Imagine God had *not* given us the capacity to feel the strong emotions of guilt and shame. Without them, how likely would we be to return to Him in worship and experience intimacy with Him in a fallen world? What would that be like?

PRAYER PAUSE

Take a few minutes to pray together — for yourself, for each other, and for others you know who might struggle with shame. Ask God to bring you hope and genuine freedom as you explore both the "big" issues and the "little" issues with Him.

PAUSE 3_OUR STARTING POINTS

Before you launch into studying these chapters, briefly discuss two or three questions below. Don't try to reach agreement or resolution now! You'll have lots of time to explore biblical principles that relate to all of these questions as you move through the study. Also let each member respond to the last two questions (7 and 8).

1. What are some things people are typically ashamed of?
2. What is shame? Is it different from guilt? How?
3. Is shame always bad, or can it be used for good?
4. What are some examples in the news or in our culture about shame?
5. Is the shame we feel always our fault?
6. Why doesn't shame always (or ever!) go away by praying, confessing, and studying Scripture?
7. As you think about studying and discussing shame with others, you . . . (mark all that apply):

   ____ Haven't thought much about it.
   ____ Want to learn to come alongside others struggling with shame.
   ____ Think it sounds like psychobabble.
   ____ Don't struggle much with the topic, but you're interested in taking a closer look.
   ____ Know what it is to struggle with shame.
   ____ Other? _____

8. Skim through this book and select one image that particularly connects with you when you think of shame. Describe briefly how that picture speaks to you.

There's no getting around it. Shame is uncomfortable. But God is in the business of taking uncomfortable things in our lives and redeeming them for our good. Consider Joseph's words to his brothers who had abused him horribly years earlier:

GENESIS 50:20. *You intended to harm me, but God intended it for good to accomplish what is now being done, the saving of many lives.*

Can you think of an example where God took something shameful in someone's life and worked good out of it? Explain.

EXAMPLE: *Chuck Colson (an assistant to President Nixon) went to jail for his crimes. But there he met Christ and now ministers effectively among prisoners.*

Every day as you read or listen to the news, be on the lookout for the impact of shame in the stories. Cut out or print any news items that illustrate people acting out of some kind of shame. Each week, bring articles you find to your group for discussion. Here's an example:

"A SENSE OF SHAME, GUILT"

Shame in The News

By Karen Rouse, *Denver Post* Staff Writer, April 22, 2007

As metro-area residents lit candles Sunday, uttered prayers and read out loud the names of the 32 people killed at Virginia Tech, many in the local Korean-American community considered the role of culture and society in the shootings. The shooter . . . emigrated to the United States from South Korea as a boy. . . .

Korean-American church members said they were astounded and ashamed as a community by Cho's actions. They described themselves as a quiet people who work hard and care about their image. When Cho gunned down the students and professors, it harmed the Korean community internationally and sparked fears of retaliation, they said.

Andre Moon, 18, said, "There is a sense of shame and guilt there for the Korean community" because Cho was from South Korea. His mother, Yeon Moon, said she believes "95 percent of Koreans feel the same way. They feel bad."

**Jot down your observations
about shame:**

PAUSE 4_BREAKING THE POWER OF SHAME

In Pause 4 of each chapter, you'll find several features:

- A key idea to apply
- A Voices of Mercy experience to do together
- A summary of key ideas from the chapter
- Suggested Scripture memory verse

KEY THOUGHTS:

- The world of shame can be complex and confusing, but hope and freedom are possible.
- Shame is a universal human experience, ranging from mild embarrassment over something as small as bad breath to humiliation over something as traumatic as sexual abuse.
- Shame comes with a whole family of emotions, such as feeling degraded, different, flawed, inadequate, worthless.
- God can redeem our shame and use it for our good.

SCRIPTURE MEMORY

Take a moment and consider the opportunity to memorize a key verse from each chapter — something you may never have tried before. You'll never regret storing these powerful verses in your heart.

It's really quite easy! Just repeat one phrase at a time and keep adding phrases until you have it all. Speaking the phrases out loud is a real help.

Take a few minutes to read together the Scripture memory overview found on page 149. This will help your group decide whether or not you'd like to make this practice a regular part of your group time. Either way, try to memorize the verse on the following page as your guiding verse for the whole study. Use the simple tips now as you memorize this verse out loud together as a group.

SUGGESTED MEMORY VERSE
FOR THIS CHAPTER

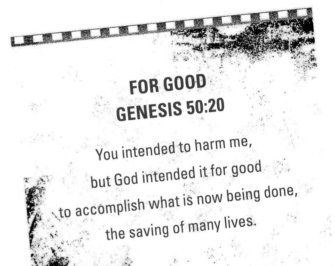

FOR GOOD
GENESIS 50:20

You intended to harm me,
but God intended it for good
to accomplish what is now being done,
the saving of many lives.

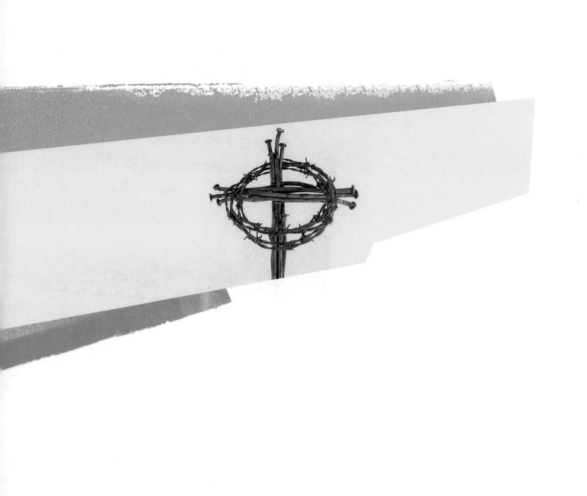

CHAPTER 2
WALKING THROUGH SHAME

Sam has asked for forgiveness more times than he can count. That October twilight when he was only nineteen has marked his heart forever. For sure, he was going a little over the speed limit, but he wasn't drunk. He wasn't trying to kill anyone. But that night his sister paid the price for his overreaction to a deer that ran in front of his car. The deer lived. He lived. But his sister died.

Sam's family and friends told him how sorry they were. That it wasn't his fault. That accidents happen. That they still loved him. But he's convinced that he doesn't deserve to really be loved by anyone — not his parents, not his friends, not his wife, and certainly not by God. Shame still whispers, "You deserve condemnation — not love!" Nothing can erase the reality of what he has done — not confession, not remorse, not even an ocean of private tears.

— Adapted from *The Shame Exchange: Trading Shame for God's Mercy and Freedom* by
Steve & Sally Breedlove and Ralph & Jennifer Ennis

What was Sam ashamed of?

Can you identify with him in any way? If so, how?

PAUSE 1_PETER'S JOURNEY INTO SHAME

Before we explore how the whole shame thing began, let's get an overview of what a journey through shame can look like and the hope that can be found on the way. One of Jesus' closest friends made this journey and his story shows us that, if we are willing to face our shame, we can find mercy in the presence of Jesus.

SCENE 1: PETER MEETS JESUS FOR THE FIRST TIME

Peter was a wild man before and after Jesus turned his life upside down. Passion, guilt, faith, shame — there was nothing tame about him. We'll look at three scenes from his story to trace Peter's walk through shame into God's mercy. From your Bible, read LUKE 5:1-11 where Peter meets Jesus for the first time.

Peter was a professional fisherman; Jesus was a carpenter. What do you imagine Peter thought at first about Jesus giving him fishing advice?

What do you think made Peter want to pull away from Jesus (verse 8)?

Is there anything in your life that sometimes makes you want to tell Jesus to, "Go away from me, for I am a sinful person"? Explain.

SCENE 2: PETER DENIES JESUS

Now fast-forward three years. Peter had spent those years living with Jesus and being changed by his experience. Scene 2 occurred the night when Peter's world would be rocked. Read LUKE 22:31-34,54-62 when Jesus warns Peter that he will deny Him three times in the coming hours.

Try putting yourself in Peter's place. Why do you think he denied knowing Jesus?

When Jesus looked him in the eyes right after his betrayal, Scripture tells us that Peter "wept bitterly" (verse 62). What self-talk or emotions do you think were going on inside Peter? Try writing what you think Peter might have written about this moment in his journal.

Parents sometimes tell their kids, "You should be ashamed of yourself." Do you think there really are times when we ought to be ashamed of ourselves? Explain.

Have you ever done something like Peter did — betrayed a friend or turned your back on someone you cared about? If so, what have you done with the shame of that event?

SCENE 3: PETER MEETS JESUS AGAIN

Peter didn't stop making bad decisions simply because he knew Jesus. But the impact of shame on Peter enabled him to receive Jesus' love and mercy in the midst of his failure. In scene 3 Peter goes back to fishing. The resurrected Jesus visits him again on the seashore. Read the story in JOHN 21:3-14 and notice how Peter responded to Jesus differently than in scene 1, despite the shame of his denial.

What is the difference in Peter's responses?

What had changed? Why did Peter want to be close to Jesus instead of pulling away as he had done earlier?

What do you think Peter learned from these experiences . . .

About himself and his shame?

About Jesus?

Imagine, if you can, jumping into the water of your shame (like Peter) and swimming toward the presence of Jesus instead of shrinking back or hiding. What might that feel like for you?

PAUSE 2_VOICES OF CONDEMNATION

Peter was probably getting slammed with shame messages from all sides — from other people, from Satan, and from his own heart. Read this passage to discover who is behind it all — who is a deadly source of condemnation and accusation:

> *REVELATION 12:10-11*
>
> *¹⁰"Then I heard a loud voice in heaven say:*
>
> *'Now have come the salvation and the power and*
> *the kingdom of our God,*
> *and the authority of his Christ.*
> *For the accuser of our brothers,*
> *who accuses them before our God day and*
> *night,*
> *has been hurled down.*
> *¹¹They overcame him*
> *by the blood of the Lamb*
> *and by the word of their testimony;*
> *they did not love their lives so much*
> *as to shrink from death.'"*

Have you ever considered what part Satan might be playing in condemning or shaming you? Why would he do that? Explain.

How does the Enemy use our shame to keep us from God?

What two things can overcome Satan's power? (verse 11)

From REVELATION 12:10-11 above, try to explain what you think Jesus' suffering, death, and resurrection all have to do with overcoming Satan's power and the power of shame.

Over the years, I have come to realize that the greatest trap in our life is not success, popularity, or power, but self-rejection. . . . As soon as someone accuses me or criticizes me, as soon as I am rejected, left alone, or abandoned, I find myself thinking, "Well, that proves once again that I am a nobody." . . . (My dark side says) "I am no good. . . . I deserve to be pushed aside, forgotten, rejected, and abandoned." Self-rejection is the greatest enemy of the spiritual life because it contradicts the sacred voice that calls us the "Beloved." Being the Beloved constitutes the core truth of our existence.

— HENRI NOUWEN, *LIFE OF THE BELOVED*

Why do you think self-rejection (the result of shame) can be such a dangerous trap in our lives?

One of Satan's most effective strategies is to get us to condemn and shame ourselves. What are one or two messages that your heart sends you when you are condemning yourself?

Consider how God responds when we condemn ourselves:

> *1 JOHN 3:19-20. This then is how we know that we belong to the truth, and how we set our hearts at rest in his presence whenever our hearts condemn us. For God is greater than our hearts, and he knows everything.*

From these verses, what is God's attitude (or what might He say) when He hears us condemning ourselves?

How can we be "at rest in his presence" even when our hearts condemn us?

God is greater than your heart. He knows everything about you (even the very worst about you!). Yet He offers you mercy in exchange for your shame.

> ROMANS 8:1-2. *Therefore, there is now no condemnation for those who are in Christ Jesus, because through Christ Jesus the law of the Spirit of life set me free from the law of sin and death.*

How does this comfort you or make you feel?

PAU/E 3_THE LANGUAGE OF /HAMING

Did you know that shame has its own language? Anyone who has called somebody an idiot or said, "Shame on you!" or uttered a curse, sexist comment, or ethnic slur speaks this language.

What shaming words have been carelessly hurled at you? Have you heard them directed at someone else, especially children (think of bullies on the playground)? Write them below.

Our verbal arsenal is loaded with contemptuous terms, some with sexual, racial, or cultural bearing, others just personally degrading. They should never be uttered. . . . Excuse the crudity, but the nearest equivalent of the biblical fool in today's language would be something more like stupid bastard or f------ jerk.

— DALLAS WILLARD, *THE DIVINE CONSPIRACY*

Consider Jesus' words about shaming language:

> *MATTHEW 5:21-22. You're familiar with the command to the ancients, "Do not murder." I'm telling you that anyone who is so much as angry with a brother or sister is guilty of murder. Carelessly call a brother "idiot!" ["fool" in NIV], and you just might find yourself hauled into court. Thoughtlessly yell "stupid!" at a sister and you are on the brink of hellfire. The simple moral fact is that words kill.* (MSG)

Jesus came down really hard on name-calling and cursing. In fact, He compared them to killing. What do you think name-calling and killing have in common?

In many families, as well as in many cultures, expression of such feelings as anger, fear, sadness or vulnerability, may be met with shaming reproaches. . . . Often these shaming admonitions are internalized, so that when we get in touch with any of these "shameful feelings" we will automatically feel shame, and try to control or hide the feelings, or, at the very least, to apologize profusely for them.

— www.columbiapsych.com/shame_miller.html

There's nothing shameful about legitimate feelings like fear, sadness, or vulnerability — though you may have been taught that. What typical "shaming" messages might send these feelings into hiding?

- *"Stop crying or I'll give you something to cry about."*

-

-

-

How (if at all) have shaming comments like those above impacted you?

God brought Peter a long way in his healing journey from shame!

> *1 PETER 3:8-9. Finally, all of you should be of one mind. Sympathize with each other. Love each other as brothers and sisters. Be tenderhearted, and keep a humble attitude. Don't repay evil for evil. Don't retaliate with insults when people insult you. Instead, pay them back with a blessing. That is what God has called you to do, and he will bless you for it.* (NLT)

According to Peter, how should we respond when others use shaming language about us or in our presence?

PAUSE 4_ BREAKING THE POWER OF SHAME

VOICES OF MERCY

We've all experienced condemnation and shame at times. They can come from our own hearts, from other people, or from Satan. As we try to resist the Accuser, we realize we're not strong enough by ourselves and shouldn't deal with it alone. But sometimes God's tender messages of mercy are blocked because we imagine Him angry and disappointed with us. We need to hear and receive God's loving messages of mercy through the lips and kindness of other people.

So in each chapter you'll find something in PAUSE 4 that invites you to actively resist those messages of condemnation and the language of shaming you may have heard in your past and to replace them with God's messages of mercy and language of blessing spoken through your group members. Your group can decide how you'd like to do this activity. You could:

1. Go around the circle. Each person speaks the following words from Scripture to the person on his/her right.
2. In pairs, read the Scriptures to each other out loud.

The point is for one person to speak sincerely, and the other to listen and receive those words as though Jesus were right there looking into their eyes. We've personalized the verses slightly by using "you" instead of "they" or "me." Feel free to insert the person's name any place, too. The verses for this chapter call you out of condemnation into a deep heart-rest in God's presence. Say to each other:

1 JOHN 3:19-20. _____ (Person's name), this then is how you can know that you belong to the truth, and how you can set your heart at rest in his presence whenever your heart condemns you. For God is greater than your heart, _____, and he knows everything. . . . It's also the way to shut down debilitating self-criticism, even when there is something to it. For God is greater than your worried heart and He knows more about you than you do yourself, _____. (MSG and NIV, personalized)

ROMANS 8:1-2. Therefore, _____ (Person's name), there is now no condemnation for you because you are in Christ Jesus, and because through Christ Jesus the law of the Spirit of life has set you free,_____, from the law of sin and death. (NIV, personalized)

KEY THOUGHTS:

- Shame can cause us to move away from Jesus or to draw close to Him.
- Condemnation and shame can come from our own hearts, from other people, and from Satan.
- Shame has its own language of demeaning words and rebukes.
- Because of the finished work of Christ, it is possible to break the power of shame and rest in God's presence.
- Breaking the power of shame involves listening more to God's voice of love and mercy than to other voices of condemnation.

SUGGESTED MEMORY VERSE FOR THIS CHAPTER

REST FROM SELF-CONDEMNATION
1 JOHN 3:19-20 (NIV)

This then is how you can know
that you belong to the truth,
and how you can set your heart
at rest in his presence
whenever your heart condemns you.
For God is greater than your heart,
and he knows everything.

CHAPTER 3
HIDING IN SHAME

Before Sara and Dan got married, they lived together for a couple of years. Back then, aborting their first child seemed like the sensible thing to do. They thought that time and marriage would wash away the guilt. But it is still there, along with shame and anger. They know they're keeping God at a distance. But now with another baby on the way, Sara can't stop crying. Family and friends don't understand her sadness and Dan's detachment — keeping their shameful secret hidden is becoming more and more difficult. The couple wants to draw near to God again, but they feel they've disgraced God. Why would He want them back?

What were Sara and Dan ashamed of?

How did they try to manage or hide their shame?

Can you identify with them in any way? If so, how?

PAUSE 1_THE BIRTH OF GUILT AND SHAME

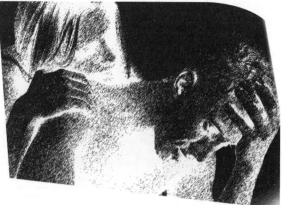

Let's go back in time to the birth of guilt and shame. Did you ever wonder where they came from originally? It all started when Adam and Eve broke the only command God had given them. When they broke His law (and His heart), they knew they deserved punishment. So they hid from Him. We still use that same old strategy to cover our guilt and shame — hiding. Read Adam and Eve's story in GENESIS 2:25–3:13,21.

Explain what you think it means that Adam and Eve were "naked and they felt no shame" (GENESIS 2:25, TNIV).

To be delivered from our phantom existence, we must drink the disgusting cup. We must quit blaming others, pretending, running, sewing fig leaves, . . . and our countless ruses by which we deny the reality of our identity. We must admit who we really are. It goes against all friendly advice . . . but in the end, the way to deepest happiness is through honest shame.

— STEVE & SALLY BREEDLOVE AND RALPH & JENNIFER ENNIS,
THE SHAME EXCHANGE: TRADING SHAME FOR GOD'S MERCY AND FREEDOM

Why did Adam and Eve experience guilt for what they had done?

Why do you think Adam and Eve felt ashamed of themselves?

HOW DID ADAM AND EVE HANDLE THEIR GUILT AND SHAME?	HOW DID GOD HANDLE THEIR GUILT AND SHAME?
Verse 7	Verse 9
Verse 8	Verses 14-19 *He explained the painful consequences of their sinful choices.*
Verses 12-13	Verse 21

When Adam and Eve violated God's command and then refused to take responsibility for that sin, they experienced the shame of their own nakedness. This shame, this self-perception of embarrassment and being "dirty," prompted them to fashion a mask from fig leaves to hide what was true about them. They were the first to try to give the appearance that they were someone other than who they actually were!

—BILL THRALL, BRUCE MCNICOL, AND JOHN LYNCH, *TRUEFACED*

WHAT DO GOD'S RESPONSES REVEAL ABOUT HIS HEART FOR ADAM AND EVE?

Imagine . . . what if God had not called out to Adam and Eve when they were hiding from Him? What if God had just left them alone to try to "fix" their feelings of shame by themselves? Describe what you think would have happened to them.

Before Jesus can break the power of our shame, we have to face whatever is causing it. What do you think is true or real about the shame that we all share with Adam and Eve?

Have you ever enjoyed a relationship where you could be soul-naked (open, vulnerable, known, be yourself) most of the time and not feel ashamed? If not, would you like to? Explain.

PAUSE 2_
GUILT AND SHAME: DESTRUCTIVE OR REDEMPTIVE?

We all feel the pain of being born into a fallen world, and we all suffer from the consequences of Adam and Eve's sin — including the capacity to experience both guilt and shame. As a result we feel separated from God.

GUILT and SHAME are closely related, but they're not the same. Both serve as "lenses," or filters, through which we view and experience sin. When we've done something wrong, our conscience makes us aware of it — we feel a sense of guilt and regret because we've broken a rule or violated a personal standard. We know we deserve some kind of punishment.

Shame introduces a sense of being a bad person, unworthiness, embarrassment, or disgrace. If we don't deal with our shame, we may become convinced that we are hopelessly flawed. This can become a root belief. Or we may go to the other extreme of "searing" our conscience and believing we're completely shameless. And those core beliefs color everything — the way sunglasses make everything look dark. We begin to let shame define who we are!

Shame is often confused with guilt, but these emotions have very different meanings. Shame is about who we are, while guilt is about what we do. . . . When we feel guilt, we expect retribution [punishment] for what we've done. When we feel shame, we expect contempt from others and feel contempt for ourselves.

— DR. RICHARD MOSKOVITZ, www.soulselfhelp.on.ca/drm10shame.html.

From what you've just read, try to distinguish between guilt and shame with a few bullet points.

GUILT	SHAME
• *Is about what we do (bad deed)*	•
•	•
•	•

JOB 10:15 may help us see shame and guilt together, as implied in this verse. Try <u>paraphrasing this verse in your own words:</u>

IN YOUR OWN WORDS. . .

If I am guilty — woe to me!
Even if I am innocent,
I cannot lift my head,
for I am full of shame
and drowned in my affliction.

Do you think Adam and Eve (and the rest of the human race) would be better off or worse off if they couldn't experience guilt and shame? Explain.

Consider how God wants to use guilt.

> JOHN 16:8. And when he [God's Holy Spirit] comes, he will convict the world of its sin, and of God's righteousness, and of the coming judgment. (NLT)

When we feel guilty, what potential good can come out of that?

What about you? Have you ever damaged a relationship and been left alone or abandoned in your shame with no one to come after you? If so, describe how that felt to you:

What connections do you see between hiding our junk and being lonely?

Because we're afraid that others won't love us if they know what's really inside us, we hide our junk. But hiding the junk also hides who we are, which keeps us more separated from love than our revealed junk ever could! . . . Maskwearers are the loneliest people on the planet.

— BILL THRALL, BRUCE MCNICOL, AND JOHN LYNCH, *TRUEFACED*

Have you felt ashamed in the last few days or weeks? If so, when and why? So what are you doing with that? Is it drawing you closer to Jesus or is it still making you feel isolated and condemned? Don't write about these questions. Instead take them to God for a few minutes.

In fact, it is necessary to have the feeling of shame if one is to be truly human. . . . Shame tells us of our limits. Shame keeps us in our human boundaries, letting us know we can and will make mistakes, and that we need help. Our shame tells us we are not God.

— JOHN BRADSHAW, *HEALING THE SHAME THAT BINDS YOU*

A MOMENT WITH GOD

The first step in redeeming our shame is to confess our sin, as David did in Psalm 51. As you read his words of confession, allow them to shape your own prayer.

PSALM 51:4-6. You're the One I've violated, and you've seen it all, seen the full extent of my evil. You have all the facts before you; whatever you decide about me is fair. I've been out of step with you for a long time, in the wrong since before I was born. What you're after is truth from the inside out. Enter me, then; conceive a new, true life. (MSG)

PAUSE 3_WAYS OF HIDING GUILT AND SHAME

There's no getting around it. All of us *are* guilty and feel some level of shame at times. These are such powerful emotions that we will do almost anything to cover them up. We'd much rather project a cleaned-up image for others than risk being seen as we really are.

So we resort to our preferred hiding styles. Sometimes we deny or minimize our shame, blame somebody else, or wallow in self-contempt. And when all else fails, we may just go numb, give up, and become shameless. Like the fig leaves that Adam and Eve used to cover their shame, the masks we choose only work for a while, if at all. But in the end, hiding just buries the screaming shame alive.

Guilt and Shame

> We know we're flawed, but instead of asking for a solution from God, whom we have offended, we try to look good, projecting a beautiful image. We concentrate on posturing, shifting the focus from ourselves by blaming others, pointing out their nakedness while desperately reaching for the fig-leaf costume hanging in our own closet.
>
> — STEVE & SALLY BREEDLOVE AND RALPH & JENNIFER ENNIS,
> *THE SHAME EXCHANGE: TRADING SHAME FOR GOD'S MERCY AND FREEDOM*

If you could add to or change anything to the above diagram to better express your experience, what would it be?

Breaking the power of shame involves identifying our preferred hiding styles and then taking courageous steps out of hiding into the light. Consider these different ways we might try to cover our shame. As you read, <u>mark</u> or highlight anything that you see as <u>a pattern in your life</u>.

HIDING STYLE	DESCRIBED	ILLUSTRATED
1. Achievement	Overachieving or overworking	• Working 60 hours a week • Competing, trying to be best
2. Anesthetizing	Numbing pain or trying to fill the emptiness with things that don't satisfy	• Abusing drugs, alcohol, food, or other addictions • Ignoring and avoiding our shame • Pornography, masturbation, or other sexual behaviors
3. Approval	Pleasing people to feel good about ourselves	• Being whatever others want us to be • Can't say no
4. Activity	Staying busy all the time	• Can't relax or be alone • Excessive religious or other activities
5. Another god (Idolatry)	Trusting anything or anyone more than God	• Materialistic or money-hungry • Trusting science to solve all problems
6. Adrenaline	Doing high-risk activities to get a rush	• Fast cars • Extreme stunts • Gambling or "get rich" schemes
7. Attention	Demanding attention from others	• Acting out • Manipulating people with our needs
8. Attacking	Overly blaming or criticizing self or others	• Cutting, self-hatred • Abusive, mean, or superior attitude • Curses, ethnic slurs, sexist comments
9. Anger	Maintaining a demanding or offensive edge	• Outbursts of rage or simmering irritation • Passive-aggressive behavior
10. Apathy	Disconnecting from life	• "Who cares? Nothing matters." • No long-range plans; cynical about future • Avoids commitments
11. _____	(Other hiding strategy?)	• •

Now review any hiding patterns you've used. Then explain one thing you marked and why.

Of course many other factors can contribute to these behaviors. But how do you think the factor of shame might have influenced your choice of hiding styles?

Do you believe most of us can overcome these behaviors and resolve our shame by ourselves if we just try harder? Explain.

Read 1 JOHN 1:5-10.

When we take the risk to confess our sins and shame to God and to others, how is that experience like walking out of darkness into light?

Now look at verses 6-7 below.

1 JOHN 1:6-7. If we claim that we experience a shared life with him and continue to stumble around in the dark, we're obviously lying through our teeth — we're not living what we claim. But if we walk in the light, God himself being the light, we also experience a shared life with one another, as the sacrificed blood of Jesus, God's Son, purges all our sin. (MSG)

From this passage, what is at the heart of a shared life with God and with others?

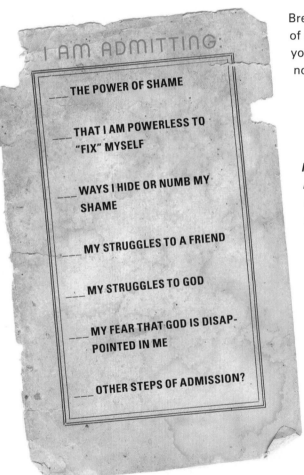

I AM ADMITTING:

____ THE POWER OF SHAME

____ THAT I AM POWERLESS TO "FIX" MYSELF

____ WAYS I HIDE OR NUMB MY SHAME

____ MY STRUGGLES TO A FRIEND

____ MY STRUGGLES TO GOD

____ MY FEAR THAT GOD IS DISAPPOINTED IN ME

____ OTHER STEPS OF ADMISSION?

Breaking the power of shame is a process of admitting several things. Where do you think you are in this process right now? Check any that apply:

NOTE: It is important not to criticize your need for hiding strategies. They served a purpose to protect you from your shame or inadequacy before you were able to look inside or receive God's mercy. For most of us, abandoning our hiding styles to God is a process that takes some time. As God heals, you won't need those old hiding styles as much as you used to.

PAUSE 4_ BREAKING THE POWER OF SHAME

Historical Background: Isaiah lived during a period when his people, the Israelites, were in moral decay and deep rebellion against God. They had every reason to *feel* guilty because they *were* guilty of great sins and idolatry. Yet Isaiah looked forward to a time when God would rescue them from their guilt and the shame they had brought on themselves and on Him. As you meditate, remember that He is still the same God who has the power to redeem you from whatever guilt and shame you carry.

Read through this passage twice.

FIRST TIME: underline words that describe how God's people felt in their guilt and shame.

SECOND TIME: circle or highlight words or phrases that describe how God responded to their shame.

ISAIAH 41:8-14

> 8 *"But you, O Israel, my servant,*
> *Jacob, whom I have chosen,*
> *you descendants of Abraham my friend,*
> 9 *I took you from the ends of the earth,*
> *from its farthest corners I called you.*
> *I said, 'You are my servant';*
> *I have chosen you and have not rejected you.*
> 10 *So do not fear, for I am with you;*
> *do not be dismayed, for I am your God.*
> *I will strengthen you and help you;*
> *I will uphold you with my righteous right hand.*
>
> 11 *"All who rage against you*
> *will surely be ashamed and disgraced;*
> *those who oppose you*
> *will be as nothing and perish.*
> 12 *Though you search for your enemies,*
> *you will not find them.*
> *Those who wage war against you*
> *will be as nothing at all.*

13 For I am the LORD, your God,

who takes hold of your right hand

and says to you, Do not fear;

I will help you.

14 Do not be afraid, O worm Jacob,

O little Israel,

for I myself will help you," declares the LORD,

your Redeemer, the Holy One of Israel.

From this passage what touches you most about God's heart?

VOICE♩ OF MERCY

As you did in the last chapter, close your group time by speaking these words of God's tender mercy into one another's hearts — either in pairs or going around the circle. As these words are spoken to you, receive them as your Father's words to you personally.

ISAIAH 41:9-14

God says, _____ (person's name), I have chosen you and have not rejected you.

10So do not fear, for I am with you; do not be dismayed, for I am your God.

I will strengthen you and help you; I will uphold you with my righteous right hand.

11 All who rage against you, _____, will surely be ashamed and disgraced;

Those who oppose you will be as nothing and perish.

13 For I am the LORD, your God, who takes hold of your right hand

and says to you, Do not fear; I will help you.

14Do not be afraid, _____ (person's name), for I myself will help you," declares the LORD, your Redeemer, the Holy One of Israel. (NIV, personalized)

KEY THOUGHTS:

- Shame usually sends us into hiding so people won't see how flawed we are.
- Breaking the power of shame involves admitting and abandoning our hiding styles.
- It also involves bringing our shame into the light of biblical community where trusted others can care, pray, guide and deeply connect with us.
- Shame can remind us that we need to receive God's solution for our flawed condition because we can't fix ourselves.
- God reaches out to us in our powerlessness and shame and offers His mercy to cover us; He invites us into relationship with Him when we feel like hiding.

SUGGESTED MEMORY VERSE FOR THIS CHAPTER

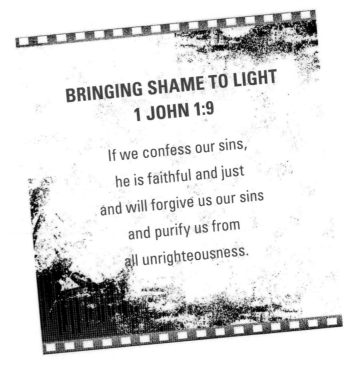

BRINGING SHAME TO LIGHT
1 JOHN 1:9

If we confess our sins,
he is faithful and just
and will forgive us our sins
and purify us from
all unrighteousness.

CHAPTER 4
SHAMED BY OTHERS

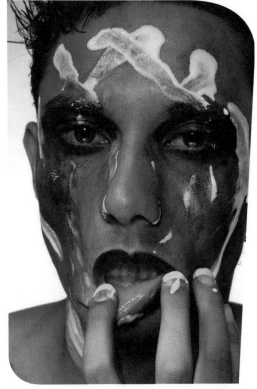

It happened during an innocent game of hide-and-seek with the neighborhood kids when he was only nine. Mateo hid in a closet with the teenager from next door. When they were found, the teenager was caught molesting him. Mateo's father was a pastor who said at the time that they should just ignore it in the name of forgiveness. Ten painful years have passed since his family swept it under the carpet and Mateo is still angry that his dad didn't stand up for him. His head knows he didn't deserve all this. But his heart feels so dirty, so soul-ugly. Maybe his other Father is ashamed of him, too.

How is Mateo's shame affecting him?

Can you identify with him in any way? If so, how?

PAUSE 1_AMNON'S ABUSE

One of the most tragic stories in the Bible describes when David's daughter Tamar was raped by her half-brother Amnon. Without flinching, God's Word explores the impact of the shame we feel when someone does something bad to us. The perpetrator deserves to feel ashamed, but too often it is the victim who walks around smothered by undeserved shame.

For some, the roots of bad shame go deep. They reach back to early abuse and abandonment, to long-standing tendencies like addiction and homosexuality, even back to centuries-old expressions of cultural and ethnic shame. For such people, bad shame rests like a thick smog upon their souls, obscuring the light of healing that Christ shines upon them.

— ANDREW COMISKEY, *STRENGTH IN WEAKNESS*

As you read this story in 2 SAMUEL 13:1-22, try to enter into Tamar's emotional world of feeling disgraced, when it should have been Amnon who felt ashamed. Write down whatever <u>emotions</u> you think each character might have felt.

Amnon

Tamar

David

Absalom

Do you think Amnon ever loved Tamar? Explain.

How did he show contempt for her?

While shame has many roots, it is a natural consequence of abuse and neglect. What all forms of abuse have in common is the contempt that an abuser has for a victim. The deeper pain of being abused is the shame that derives from being an object of contempt. Many abusers show their contempt explicitly in the form of degrading words, but all abusers show contempt by their assumption that their victim's primary role is as an instrument for their gratification.

— WWW.SOULSELFHELP.ON.CA

PAUSE 2_AMNON'S SHAMELESSNESS

What role did Jonadab play in Amnon's shameless behavior?

How can our peers "shame" us into shameless behavior? Try to think of an example.

When our hiding strategies don't work anymore, some of us give up the struggle and just become shameless, like Amnon.

> JEREMIAH 6:15
> "Are they ashamed of their loathsome conduct?
>   No, they have no shame at all;
>   they do not even know how to blush.
>   So they will fall among the fallen;
>   they will be brought down when I punish them,"
>   says the LORD.

Try to describe what it means to be "shameless." Or give an example you've seen of someone acting shamelessly, from the media or real life.

What happens to people who have become so shameless that nothing makes them blush anymore? Mark whatever you see in these passages.

ROMANS 1:28-32. Furthermore, since they did not think it worthwhile to retain the knowledge of God, he gave them over to a depraved mind, to do what ought not to be done. They have become filled with every kind of wickedness, evil, greed and depravity. They are full of envy, murder, strife, deceit and malice. They are gossips, slanderers, God-haters, insolent, arrogant and boastful; they invent ways of doing evil; they disobey their parents; they are senseless, faithless, heartless, ruthless. Although they know God's righteous decree that those who do such things deserve death, they not only continue to do these very things but also approve of those who practice them.

1 TIMOTHY 4:2. By means of the hypocrisy of liars seared in their own conscience as with a branding iron. (NASB)

What happens to a conscience that has been "seared as with a branding iron"?

According to this passage, God's people couldn't respond to truth anymore. They became so shameless that He had to expose them to shame.

JEREMIAH 13:24-27. "I will scatter you like chaff that is blown away by the desert winds. This is your allotment, the portion I have assigned to you," says the LORD, "for you have forgotten me, putting your trust in false gods. I myself will strip you and expose you to shame. I have seen your adultery and lust, and your disgusting idol worship out in the fields and on the hills. What sorrow awaits you, Jerusalem! How long before you are pure?" (NLT)

In light of the last three passages you've read above, why do you think God took this drastic step to give His people a nasty taste of shame? Do you think He was being mean or merciful — or something else?

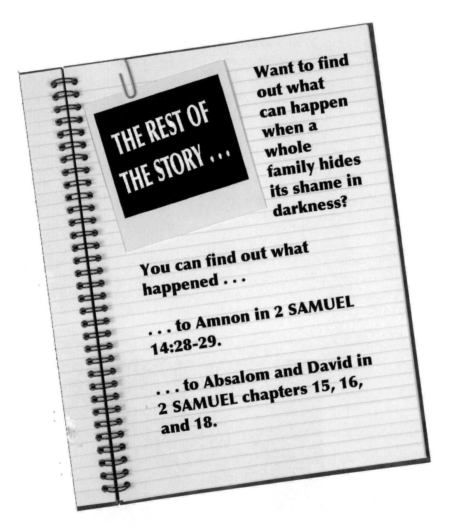

THE REST OF THE STORY . . .

Want to find out what can happen when a whole family hides its shame in darkness?

You can find out what happened . . .

. . . to Amnon in 2 SAMUEL 14:28-29.

. . . to Absalom and David in 2 SAMUEL chapters 15, 16, and 18.

PAUSE 3_TAMAR'S SHAME

Shame can reveal a need that leads to good, but it can also crush us. The stories about Peter and Adam and Eve show how shame can open the door to connect with God's tender mercy. But shame can also do the opposite: It can push us into isolation from God and others by telling us we're stupid, useless, and unlovable. It's more about *being* bad than about *doing* bad. Maybe it helps to think of shame as "the raincoat of the soul."

Shame is the raincoat of the soul, repelling the living water that would otherwise establish us as the beloved of God. It prevents us from receiving grace and truth where we need them most. . . . Bad shame . . . forms a "shame coat" causing us to conclude that we are unworthy of love and honor. The emotion of inferiority, bad shame expresses itself as "an inner torment, a sickness of the soul" that divides us from self, others and God. Bad shame invites the soul to turn on itself rather than to welcome mercy. Bad shame bars us from life.

— ANDREW COMISKEY, *STRENGTH IN WEAKNESS*

Peter denied Jesus. Adam and Eve disobeyed God. Amnon raped his sister. So their shame flowed from their own sins. But Tamar's shame was different. It flowed from terrible sins committed against her and led to "a sickness of the soul."

Another injury due to victimization is a deep, pervasive sense of being "all-bad," wrong, dirty, or shameful. No matter how affirming others are of their loveableness and their attributes, victims are convinced that, underneath it all, there is no good inside themselves. . . . They take on badness that isn't theirs. They begin believing that the way they were treated is the way they should be treated.

— DR. HENRY CLOUD AND DR. JOHN TOWNSEND, *BOUNDARIES*

Tamar wasn't guilty of anything! The rape wasn't her fault. So why do you think she felt so ashamed?

How do you think Tamar felt about . . .

being raped by Amnon?

being rejected by Amnon?

Absalom's response to her? (2 SAMUEL 13:20-22)

From what we can tell, neither her father, David, nor her brother, Absalom, ever spoke to Amnon about what he had done to Tamar. How do you think the silence of her father and brother impacted Tamar?

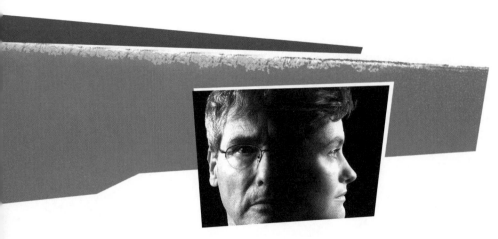

If Absalom or David could get a second chance to respond sensitively to Tamar right after her rape and really be there for her, what do you think she would have wanted them to say? Write a few sentences.

What I discovered was that shame as a healthy human emotion can be transformed into shame as a state of being. As a state of being, shame takes over one's whole identity. To have shame as an identity is to believe that one's being is flawed, that one is defective as a human being. Once shame is transformed into an identity, it becomes toxic and dehumanizing.

— JOHN BRADSHAW, *HEALING THE SHAME THAT BINDS YOU*

2 SAMUEL 13:20 describes Tamar as "a desolate woman." On your own or using a dictionary, describe what it means to feel "desolate."

Are there any areas in your life where you feel desolate? Or has someone hurt you and caused you to feel shame? Explain.

Have you ever felt like Tamar — that there was no place to go with your shame (verse 13)? Briefly describe that experience.

How do you think the silence of Mateo's family (in the opening story) may have affected him? Do you think their silence decreased or increased his pain and shame? Explain.

Imagine Jesus spending time with Mateo and Tamar. What do you imagine He might say to them?

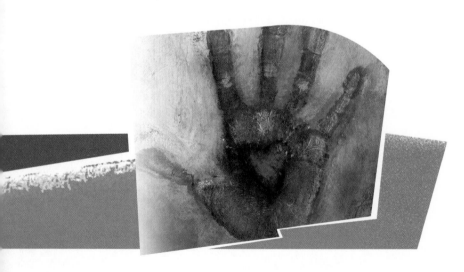

PAUƧE 4_ BREAKING THE POWER OF ƧHAME

In the following passage, God spoke to His people through the prophet Isaiah as if they were a young woman who had been disgraced and humiliated — just like Tamar. He didn't want them (and He doesn't want us) to end up like Tamar: desolate and alone. Breaking the power of shame involves bringing our shame to Him for comfort (and admitting our shame to others, as we'll see in the next chapter.)

Read this passage twice. The first time you read it, underline any words that describe how Tamar — or anyone suffering deep shame — can feel. The second time through, circle any words of comfort God offers us in our shame.

> ISAIAH 54:4-6
>
> "Do not be afraid; you will not suffer shame. Do not fear disgrace; you will not be humiliated. You will forget the shame of your youth and remember no more the reproach of your widowhood.
>
> For your Maker is your husband — the LORD Almighty is his name — the Holy One of Israel is your Redeemer; he is called the God of all the earth.
>
> The LORD will call you back as if you were a wife deserted and distressed in spirit — a wife who married young, only to be rejected," says your God.

Regardless of your gender or age or marital status, how do you connect with "the shame of your youth" or "the reproach of your widowhood" (verse 4)?

VOICES OF MERCY

As you've done before, take these words of comfort God spoke to His people and speak them to one another in your group. Your shame may tell you not to believe them. But in Christ they hold the power to wash away your shame — especially "the shame of your youth." Say these words from Isaiah to each other:

> *ISAIAH 54:4-5*
> *"Do not be afraid, _____; you will not suffer shame.*
> *Do not fear disgrace; you will not be humiliated.*
> *You will forget the shame of your youth, _____,*
> *and remember no more the reproach of your widowhood.*
> *For . . . the Holy One of Israel is your Redeemer;*
> *he is called the God of all the earth." (NIV, personalized)*

KEY THOUGHTS:

- If you are feeling chronically guilty, angry, embarrassed, disgraced, or humiliated, ask yourself if shame may be at the root.
- We may feel ashamed even when we haven't done anything wrong because of what someone else has done to us.
- How other people respond to our shame makes a big difference in whether we feel comforted or shamed even more.

SUGGESTED MEMORY VERSE
FOR THIS CHAPTER

Shame Forgotten
ISAIAH 54:4-5

Do not be afraid; you will not suffer shame.
Do not fear disgrace;
you will not be humiliated.
You will forget the shame of your youth
and remember no more the reproach
of your widowhood.
For . . . the Holy One of Israel is your Redeemer;
he is called the God of all the earth.

CHAPTER 5
TYPES OF SHAME

PREACHER'S WIFE SAYS SHE WAS ABUSED

Selmer, Tenn. — A preacher's wife testified at her murder trial Wednesday that her husband abused her physically and sexually, but she said the shotgun fired accidentally as she pointed it at him in their parsonage bedroom. Mary Winkler testified her husband punched her in the face, kicked her at times and refused to grant her a divorce.

Speaking about their sex life, she spoke quietly and hesitantly, with eyes downcast. She said Matthew Winkler forced her to view pornography, dress "slutty" and have sex she considered unnatural. Pornographic photos she identified as coming from their home computer were entered as evidence.

"I was ashamed," she said, explaining why she told no one of the abuse. "I didn't want anybody to know about Matthew."

— Excerpted from The Denver Post, Thursday, April 19, 2007

Shame in The News

What if . . . ? If we could ask Matthew Winkler why he didn't get help for his struggles, what do you think he might say? What might Mary Winkler say?

What if either Matthew or Mary had come into the light and sought out help? How do you think this story might have ended differently?

Can you relate in any way to this story?

PAUƧE 1_AN INVIƧIBLE WOMAN

Shame is sometimes linked with a feeling of powerlessness. We may think, *Something about me is flawed and I'm powerless to change it.* Maybe it's a physical handicap or emotional wounding of some kind. An unnamed woman in the story below from the gospel of Mark had several reasons to feel shame.

Cultural Background: *Jewish Old Testament law made it hard for women during their monthly period. Any discharge of blood made a woman — as well as anyone and almost anything she touched — ceremonially "unclean" for up to seven days. Married women had it even harder. Jewish law prohibited all physical contact (including sex) between a husband and wife during such times. They couldn't pass objects to each other, sit on the same surface, sleep in the same bed, eat from the same plate, or see each other undressed.*

PART 1: MARK 5:24-29

> *24 Jesus went with him, and all the people followed, crowding around him. 25 A woman in the crowd had suffered for twelve years with constant bleeding. 26 She had suffered a great deal from many doctors, and over the years she had spent everything she had to pay them, but she had gotten no better. In fact, she had gotten worse. 27 She had heard about Jesus, so she came up behind him through the crowd and touched his robe. 28 For she thought to herself, "If I can just touch his robe, I will be healed." 29 Immediately the bleeding stopped, and she could feel in her body that she had been healed of her terrible condition.* (NLT)

Verses 24-25: How do you think the people in the crowd might have felt being pressed against the woman considered "unclean" or maybe immoral? (See JOHN 9:1-3.)

Verse 26: It is very possible that she had never married or had lost her husband because of her constant discharge. Try to list five (or more) things she had probably lost because of her illness.

PART 2: MARK 5:30-34

> [30] *Jesus realized at once that healing power had gone out from him, so he turned around in the crowd and asked, "Who touched my robe?"*
>   [31] *His disciples said to him, "Look at this crowd pressing around you. How can you ask, 'Who touched me?'"*
>   [32] *But he kept on looking around to see who had done it.* [33] *Then the frightened woman, trembling at the realization of what had happened to her, came and fell to her knees in front of him and told him what she had done.* [34] *And he said to her, "Daughter, your faith has made you well. Go in peace. Your suffering is over."* (NLT)

Verses 30-32: This woman's story doesn't end at verse 29! Why do you think Jesus insisted on publicly identifying the person who touched him? Was He shaming her again — or something else?

Verse 34: Jesus healed more than a chronically ill body — he healed her felt need. What other deep needs in her life did Jesus heal that day? Think about any differences between her being "healed" (verse 29) and being "made well or whole" (verse 34).

How do you imagine her life had changed after she faced her shame and experienced mercy from Jesus?

In what ways (if at all) can you identify with this woman?

In the great shame exchange, Jesus not only took away her bleeding and her shame but He also publicly affirmed her as a model of faith (verses 27-29,34). When you come to Jesus with your shame, do you expect affirmation or blessing — or something else? Explain.

Think of the other people in your small group. What are some things you can affirm in each other as you seek to break the power of shame in your lives? If you could text message one member of your group with a word of affirmation, what would you say, and to whom?

*PAUSE 2*_ FIVE TYPES OF SHAME

As we've seen, some shame comes from our choices to sin, like Adam and Eve or Amnon. Other shame comes from others sinning against us, as in Tamar's story. A third source of shame might come from our life circumstances — like our weaknesses and failures, gender, appearance or body issues. From this list, consider five sources or types of shame. (You'll explore five more types of shame in the next chapter.)

1. **IDENTITY-LEVEL SHAME**: *experiencing being human*

   We feel the pain of being born into a fallen world and being impacted by the consequences of Adam and Eve's sin. So we feel separated from God because we fall short of His glory (Romans 3:23).

2. **VICTIM SHAME**: *experiencing abuse*

   We are violated verbally, emotionally, physically, sexually, or economically.

3. **PERFORMANCE SHAME**: *experiencing failure*

   We fail to meet our own or others' standards of success. Our shame tells us, "You're a loser, not good enough. That's why you perform so badly."

4. **IMAGE SHAME**: *experiencing loss of face*

   We lose face through public shaming, parental embarrassment, being compared with brothers or sisters or peers, being criticized at work.

5. **GENDER SHAME**: *experiencing inadequacy*

   We sense deep physical inadequacy and disgust at our own bodies as well as failing to meet standards of sexual beauty or power.

   — ADAPTED FROM *THE SHAME EXCHANGE: TRADING SHAME FOR GOD'S MERCY AND FREEDOM* BY STEVE & SALLY BREEDLOVE AND RALPH & JENNIFER ENNIS

Using the list above, what type(s) of shame might be stirred up if . . .

_____ you lost your job because you were lazy and just didn't take it seriously.

_____ you didn't make the cheerleading squad because you weren't a size 4.

_____ your dad lost his temper at your basketball game and screamed at the coach.

_____ your aunt scolded you by saying, "No wonder you act like trash — you *are* trash!"

_____ two thugs beat you up and yelled ethnic slurs at you.

_____ your wife dumped you and the baby for her old boyfriend.

_____ you stutter when you talk.

From the list above, which kinds of shame do you think might have been experienced . . .

by the Winklers in the opening story of this chapter?

by the invisible woman? (Mark 5:24-34)

What type(s) of shame from the previous list do you most identify with? Explain.

Heaped-on shame can be devastating. Sexual and verbal abuse lash the unprotected. Racial prejudice is an inherited legacy — there is nothing you can do about the way you were born. Physical deformities often cannot be corrected. The shame of being deserted by your adulterous spouse or by your father or mother stings for a lifetime. Never really succeeding in a career makes you want to hide. Your inability to find a spouse or have children can feel like it is being broadcast on every channel.

The challenge is that heaped-on shame catalyzes true identity-level shame.... Identity-level shame does have its root in our souls. We were born in sin. We are guilty before God, and that true shame must be walked toward. On the other hand, the shame that has been heaped upon us needs to be named for what it is and rejected.

It is good to spend time learning to distinguish between real identity-level shame and heaped-on shame.

— STEVE & SALLY BREEDLOVE AND RALPH & JENNIFER ENNIS, *THE SHAME EXCHANGE: TRADING SHAME FOR GOD'S MERCY AND FREEDOM*

Read this quote. Use different colors of highlighters to mark characteristics of "heaped-on" shame and "identity-level" shame. Then summarize in your own words:

HEAPED-ON SHAME:

IDENTITY-LEVEL SHAME:

If you could produce a movie or video (or paint a picture or write a book) exploring one of these types of shame, which one would you choose? Explain.

PAUSE 3_SHAME REDEEMED

Shame is real. We live in a world that is broken and degraded in many ways. It's likely that our environment or experiences have somehow brought shame into our lives. But God specializes in bringing good out of bad and hope out of brokenness. He delights in redeeming our shame.

Read the following Scriptures. Write on the chart anything you notice about God bringing beauty out of ugliness or restoring broken and hurting people.

BROKEN	REDEEMED
Brokenhearted	*Bound up*

ISAIAH 61:1-3

> The Spirit of the Sovereign LORD is on me,
> because the LORD has anointed me
> to preach good news to the poor.
> He has sent me to bind up the brokenhearted,
> to proclaim freedom for the captives
> and release from darkness for the prisoners,
>
> ² to proclaim the year of the LORD's favor
> and the day of vengeance of our God,
> to comfort all who mourn,
>
> ³ and provide for those who grieve in Zion —
> to bestow on them a crown of beauty
> instead of ashes,
> the oil of gladness
> instead of mourning,
> and a garment of praise
> instead of a spirit of despair.
> They will be called oaks of righteousness,
> a planting of the LORD
> for the display of his splendor.

2 CORINTHIANS 4:16-18. Therefore we do not lose heart. Though outwardly we are wasting away, yet inwardly we are being renewed day by day. For our light and momentary troubles are achieving for us an eternal glory that far outweighs them all. So we fix our eyes not on what is seen, but on what is unseen. For what is seen is temporary, but what is unseen is eternal.

PROTECTING YOURSELF FROM SHAME

Nobody wants to be put to shame. But how can we avoid it? Here's some practical help. From these verses, what can we do to protect ourselves from being put to shame?

> PSALM 119:80. May I be blameless in keeping your decrees; then I will never be ashamed. (NLT)

> PSALM 25:20

> PSALM 34:5

From these verses, one thing I would like to do to deal with my shame is:

A MOMENT WITH GOD

Pause to talk with God about anything that has been stirred up in you from these verses or this chapter. What are the roots of your shame? Picture yourself bringing your shame to Jesus. Tell Him how intensely you feel your sense of shame. What do you "see" God doing with your shame? What do you "hear" Him saying to you? After praying, journal here.

PAUSE 4_BREAKING THE POWER OF SHAME

VOICES OF MERCY

Our struggle against shame lasts a lifetime. So whenever shame returns to bother you, you can put those accusations in their place by reading these words out loud and believing them in your heart. The point isn't just getting a second chance (or even a ninety-second chance)! It is about being intimately connected with God. The same merciful God who promised to end the shame of His people wants to meet you on your journey, too. For now, read these words of comfort and hope out loud to one another in your group.

ZEPHANIAH 3:16-20

*¹⁶ "Cheer up, _____ (person's name)! Don't be afraid! For the L*ORD *your God is living among you. He is a mighty savior. He will take delight in you with gladness. With his love, _____ , he will calm all your fears. He will rejoice over you with joyful songs."*

*¹⁸ [Your God says] "I will gather you who mourn . . . ; you will be disgraced no more. And I will deal severely with all who have oppressed you, _____. I will save the weak and helpless ones; I will bring together those who were chased away. I will give glory and fame to my former exiles, wherever they have been mocked and shamed. On that day I will gather you together and bring you home again. I will give you a good name, a name of distinction, among all the nations of the earth, as I restore your fortunes before their very eyes. I, the L*ORD*, have spoken!" (*NLT*, personalized)*

KEY THOUGHTS:

- Sometimes shame is linked with a feeling of powerlessness.
- We might also feel bad because of the shame people heap on us related to our life circumstances such as our gender, performance, failure, appearance, bodies, or limitations.
- There's a difference between real identity-level shame and heaped-on shame in terms of its source. But both kinds can be brought to Jesus because He has the power to break shame's power over us.
- God specializes in bringing good out of bad and hope out of brokenness. He delights in redeeming our shame.

SUGGESTED MEMORY VERSE FOR THIS CHAPTER

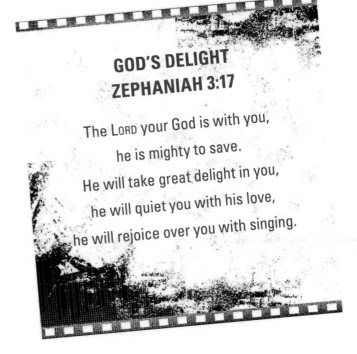

GOD'S DELIGHT
ZEPHANIAH 3:17

The LORD your God is with you,
he is mighty to save.
He will take great delight in you,
he will quiet you with his love,
he will rejoice over you with singing.

CHAPTER 6
OVERPOWERED BY SHAME

Sister Carlotta: "God gives us the freedom to do great evil, if we choose. Then he uses his own freedom to create goodness out of that evil, for that is what he chooses."

Anton (the Geneticist): "So, in the long run, God always wins."

Sister Carlotta: "Yes."

Anton: "In the short run, though, it can be uncomfortable."

Sister Carlotta: "And when, in the past, would you have preferred to die, instead of being alive here today?"

Anton: "There it is. We get used to everything. We find hope in anything."

Sister Carlotta: "That's why I've never understood suicide. Even those suffering from great depression or guilt — don't they feel Christ the Comforter in their hearts, giving them hope?"

Anton: "You're asking me?"

Sister Carlotta: "God not being convenient, I ask a fellow mortal."

Anton: "In my view, suicide is not really the wish for life to end."

Sister Carlotta: "What is it, then?"

Anton: "It is the only way a powerless person can find to make everybody else look away from his shame. The wish is not to die, but to hide."

Sister Carlotta: "As Adam and Eve hid from the Lord."

Anton: "Because they were naked."

Sister Carlotta: "If only such sad people could remember: Everyone is naked. Everyone wants to hide. But life is still sweet. Let it go on."

> — Scene from science fiction novel *Ender's Shadow*, by Orson Scott Card

Anton thinks that suicide isn't usually about wanting life to end, but rather wanting to hide — so other people won't see our shame. Do you agree or disagree? Explain.

Sister Carlotta says that everybody is naked and wants to hide something — but life is still sweet. Do you agree or disagree? Explain.

How (if at all) has your life been touched by suicide — or attempted suicide?

PAUSE 1_DYING IN SHAME

Consider the story of Judas betraying Jesus.

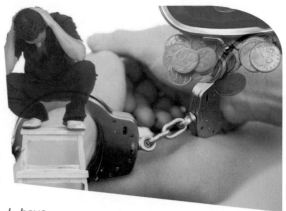

MATTHEW 27:3-10. When Judas, who had betrayed him, realized that Jesus had been condemned to die, he was filled with remorse. So he took the thirty pieces of silver back to the leading priests and the elders.

"I have sinned," he declared, "for I have betrayed an innocent man."

"What do we care?" they retorted. "That's your problem."

Then Judas threw the silver coins down in the Temple and went out and hanged himself. The leading priests picked up the coins. "It wouldn't be right to put this money in the Temple treasury," they said, "since it was payment for murder." After some discussion they finally decided to buy the potter's field, and they made it into a cemetery for foreigners. (NLT)

How did Judas die?

Try to imagine how Judas felt when he "realized that Jesus had been condemned to die [and was] filled with remorse" (verse 3). Write out what he might have said to himself just before he died.

Judas isn't the only one who turned on Jesus — Peter denied Jesus publicly several times. Yet they handled their guilt and shame very differently. From what you remember about Peter's story (see page 27), write what you imagine he told himself to do with his shame.

Who we choose to reveal our shame to makes a big difference. Remember how the priests and religious leaders responded to Judas' confession (verse 4)? Have you ever chosen to share your shame with unsafe people (as Judas did)? If so, what was their response and how did it affect you?

Whatever you struggle with, where might your shame lead you if you leave it in the dark so nobody can help you? What's at risk if you keep your stuff hidden indefinitely?

What's at risk if you bring it into the open?

Is there anyone you trust enough to see your shame and walk with you through it? What feelings get stirred up as you consider sharing your story with this person? Explain.

Like Judas, the apostle Paul had lots to be guilty and ashamed of: for starters, he tracked down people who followed Jesus and had them killed. But unlike Judas, Paul wasn't overpowered by his shame and didn't allow all that to separate him from God. No matter what he'd done, God's love was stronger than his shame.

ROMANS 8:31. What shall we say about such wonderful things as these? If God is for us, who can ever be against us? (NLT)

As you think about facing more things you are ashamed of, what are two or three things you fear?

What if you *only* try to manage your shame by yourself?

Now think about whatever you feel is separating you from God — past or present. Read ROMANS 8:38-39 in your Bible and fill in the blanks with your own words that reflect your life:

ROMANS 8:38-39. "For I am convinced that neither _____ nor _____ , neither _____ nor _____ nor anything else in all creation, will be able to separate [me] from the love of God that is in Christ Jesus our Lord." (NIV, personalized)

PAUSE 2_FIVE MORE TYPES OF SHAME

As you read about five more types of shame (continuing from chapter 5), try to think of a real-life example from your own experience (or someone you know or have heard about) for each type of shame.

6. **FAMILY SHAME:** *experiencing "being like them"*

    We're so closely tied to our families and their (sometimes unhealthy) issues that we take their shame on ourselves. We experience shame from a family member's mental illness, drug abuse, imprisonment, addictions, poverty, social standing, or appearance.

7. **CULTURAL SHAME:** *experiencing "who my people are"*

    We feel a painful sense of unfairness or embarrassment because of our racial, ethnic, national, or cultural background.

8. **SURVIVOR SHAME:** *experiencing "undeservedness"*

    We feel confused and unworthy when we survive a tragedy, disease, or accident in which others died. We ask, "Why did I survive when they died?"

9. **SOCIO-ECONOMIC SHAME:** *experiencing social or material deprivation*

    We feel left out by not having the status symbols of the rich or privileged, or we feel shamed because of our affluence or advantages

10. **"SPIRITUAL" SHAME:** *experiencing religious inadequacy or church abuse*

    We feel inferior to others spiritually, being told or telling ourselves that we don't have enough faith, have too many problems, have unconfessed sin, or aren't spiritual enough to please God.

— ADAPTED FROM *THE SHAME EXCHANGE: TRADING SHAME FOR GOD'S MERCY AND FREEDOM* BY STEVE &
SALLY BREEDLOVE AND RALPH & JENNIFER ENNIS

Using the list on the previous page, what type(s) of shame might be stirred up if . . .

_____ your debt is huge, your credit rating is terrible, and the bank is foreclosing on your condo.

_____ you're a veteran having trouble moving on and you have nightmares about your buddies who died in Iraq.

_____ you've been in treatment for an eating disorder, your brother committed suicide when he returned from the war, your mom works at the canning factory, and your family depends on food stamps.

_____ you've fasted and prayed and given lots of money to the local church — but still your brother is dying.

_____ you are the only black person and the only woman manager in your company, and you're getting harassed at work.

Is there one of the above types of shame that you can connect with personally? Explain.

Unfortunately, when Judas took his shame to the priests and religious leaders, all he got was more shame. And this still happens today. Read this story about "spiritual" abuse.

Not long ago I . . . taught a course at a seminary on how shame-based issues affect churches and families. After presenting a session on spiritual abuse, a woman approached me at the podium.

"I just can't bring myself to read the Bible anymore," she blurted. "I feel sad because God's Word used to be important to me. But now every time I try to read it I actually get an upset stomach."

After we talked a little more I discovered that she had been horribly abused with God's Word. Every time something happened to her or to anyone in her immediate family, she was referred to Scriptures about 'supernatural faith.' And she was told that if she'd been praying, 'doing spiritual warfare,' these attacks would not be getting through and harming her family.

"I guess I'm the problem, really. I don't have enough faith. I'm a weak Christian," she concluded. The anticipation of getting bad spiritual news was so great that she could no longer bring herself to read the Bible.

— PAUL HIDGON, _THE SUBTLE POWER OF SPIRITUAL ABUSE_

How (if at all) can you relate to the woman from this story?

Jesus got angry at people who abuse and shame others under the guise of religion. Mark whatever you notice about that in the passage below:

MATTHEW 23:13-15,23. "Woe to you, teachers of the law and Pharisees, you hypocrites! You shut the kingdom of heaven in men's faces. You yourselves do not enter, nor will you let those enter who are trying to. Woe to you, teachers of the law and Pharisees, you hypocrites! You travel over land and sea to win a single convert, and when he becomes one, you make him twice as much a son of hell as you are. . . . 23 Woe to you, teachers of the law and Pharisees, you hypocrites! You give a tenth of your spices — mint, dill and cumin. But you have neglected the more important matters of the law — justice, mercy and faithfulness."

Summarize what you think was Jesus' primary issue with the Pharisees in this passage.

How have you seen others hurt by unsafe religious leaders or environments? Explain.

PAUSE 3_SHAME IN THE NEWS

Not all shame is individual. Some shame is attached to whole families, cultures, nations, or systems. Mark whatever you notice about shame in this news story.

IRAQI PRISONERS PREFER DEATH TO SHAMING

The anguished Iraqi prisoner at Abu Ghraib pointed to the space between his eyes and begged his American guard to shoot him.

"Shoot me here, but don't do this to us!"

Do what? Saddam Hussein had thousands of his own people mutilated, tortured, and killed. So what were these guards doing that was worse than death?

According to an American military pamphlet, one of the worst things that can happen to an Iraqi man is to be shamed or humiliated in public. Iraqis think lots of things are "unclean" — like feet or the soles of feet, the ground, being naked or using the bathroom around others, bodily fluids, etc. Yet at Abu Ghraib, Iraqi prisoners were forced to parade around naked, put shoes in their mouths, squirm on the ground, masturbate in front of female soldiers, and pile up naked in "human pyramids" — and they were powerless to do anything about it.

But most shameful of all, it was done publicly — in front of foreigners, men and women, and a camera, to be shown over and over again long after the actual humiliation stopped.

No wonder they preferred a bullet to the head.

—ADAPTED FROM "FAMILY OF AFGHAN RAPE VICTIM DEMANDS JUSTICE," BY ALISA TANG, THE ASSOCIATED PRESS, LAST UPDATED 08/24/2007

What do you notice about cultural shame and honor in this story?

What do you think Jesus might say . . .

   to the Iraqi prisoner?

   to the American guard?

PRAYER PAUSE

Listen to what Ezra prayed about the shame of his culture and nation.

EZRA 9:6-7. My dear God, I'm so totally ashamed, I can't bear to face you. O my God — our iniquities are piled up so high that we can't see out; our guilt touches the skies. We've been stuck in a muck of guilt since the time of our ancestors until right now; we and our kings and priests, because of our sins, have been turned over to foreign kings, to killing, to captivity, to looting, and to public shame — just as you see us now. (MSG)

What are a few things about your own culture or nation that you feel ashamed of? List them here. Then take a few minutes to talk with God about that, as Ezra did.

CONSIDER HOW GOD CAN REDEEM THE BROKEN OR SHAMEFUL PARTS OF OUR LIVES.

1 CORINTHIANS 1:26-30. Remember, dear brothers and sisters, that few of you were wise in the world's eyes or powerful or wealthy when God called you. Instead, God deliberately chose things the world considers foolish in order to shame those who think they are wise. And he chose things that are powerless to shame those who are powerful. God chose things despised by the world, things counted as nothing at all, and used them to bring to nothing what the world considers important. As a result, no one can ever boast in the presence of God.

³⁰ God has united you with Christ Jesus. For our benefit God made him to be wisdom itself. Christ made us right with God; he made us pure and holy, and he freed us from sin. (NLT)

How does God's view of shame differ from the world's view?

From these passages, what encouragement does God offer to those of us who feel "foolish . . . powerless . . . despised . . . discounted"?

PAUSE 4_ BREAKING THE POWER OF SHAME

In the opening story, Sister Carlotta said, "Even those suffering from great depression or guilt — don't they feel Christ the Comforter in their hearts, giving them hope? . . . If only such sad people could remember: Everyone is naked. Everyone wants to hide. But life is still sweet. Let it go on."

How have you experienced the "sweetness of life"? Describe that.

VOICES OF MERCY

In this messed-up world, it's impossible to avoid shame entirely. But when it comes our way — whether we asked for it or not — no child of God needs to be overpowered by it. This time, go around your group with each member reading one line from this passage, slowly and out loud, to encourage each other:

> ROMANS 8:28,31-34,38-39
> And we know that in all things God works for the good of those who love him, who have been called according to his purpose. . . .
> What, then, shall we say in response to this? If God is for us, who can be against us?
> He who did not spare his own Son, but gave him up for us all — how will he not also, along with him, graciously give us all things?
> Who will bring any charge against those whom God has chosen? It is God who justifies.
> Who is he that condemns? Christ Jesus, who died — more than that, who was raised to life — is at the right hand of God and is also interceding for us. . . .
> For I am convinced that neither death nor life, neither angels nor demons, neither the present nor the future, nor any powers, neither height nor depth, nor anything else in all creation, will be able to separate us from the love of God that is in Christ Jesus our Lord.

KEY THOUGHTS:

- We all feel ashamed, naked, and want to hide at times. But life is still sweet.
- Sometimes shame makes us feel powerless. But Jesus can free us from the power of shame if we invite Him to.
- Heaped-on shame can come from a variety of sources, including family shame, cultural shame, survivor shame, socio-economic shame, and "spiritual" shame.
- Nothing, including our shame, can separate us from the love of God in Christ.

SUGGESTED MEMORY VERSE FOR THIS CHAPTER

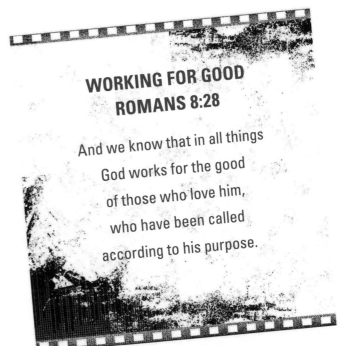

**WORKING FOR GOOD
ROMANS 8:28**

And we know that in all things
God works for the good
of those who love him,
who have been called
according to his purpose.

CHAPTER 7:
OFFERING TRUTH WITH MERCY

Sakura never thought that she would lose control and end up in prison. It started out small, taking inexpensive items — a candy bar or earrings for her new outfit. The rush she experienced when she shoplifted released her, for a moment, from the internal prison of feeling bad, stained, unworthy. But, after making the terrifying call to her family admitting the truth of her theft, the shame of embarrassing her family was even worse than the shame she felt for stealing.

So why did her brother Kaito keep seeking her out, even when she refused to take his calls? Today was the first time she had agreed to let him visit her in jail. She tried to prepare herself for the humiliation of looking through the cold security glass and the awkwardness of speaking through the telephone in the visitor center.

But nothing prepared her for Kaito's first words of tender mercy: "We love you, Sakura. We know what you did, but we're not ashamed of you. We can't wait for you to come home!" For the first time, though behind bars, she was not alone in her shame and felt the freedom to come clean about her secret addiction.

What was Sakura ashamed of?

Can you identify with her in any way? If so, how?

To experience God's grace . . . our hearts have to be connected to it. We can certainly connect to God "vertically" through prayer, but to feel his grace completely we have to be open to the full expression of it "horizontally" through other people. To connect fully with the grace of God, we have to go to where it is, and he has chosen to put it into other people.

— DR. HENRY CLOUD AND DR. JOHN TOWNSEND, *HOW PEOPLE GROW*

PAUSE 1_DAVID FACES HIS SHAME

So far in our study we have discovered that we need to experience God's mercy calling us out of
hiding. But *how* do we experience
this? Mercy isn't just ignoring bad
things. It involves having the truth about us
exposed — and that can feel absolutely terrifying. In this chapter you'll explore how truth and
mercy, together, help to restore our intimacy with God.

The time had come when King David faced some harsh truths about himself in order to taste
God's mercy. Read his story in 2 SAMUEL 11:1-27.

From this passage, how did David cover up sins and deceptions?

So God sent a friend named Nathan to help David through this critical time of moral failure
and personal crisis. Read about their relationship and David's restoration in 2 SAMUEL 12:1-
14 and 24-25.

How did God use Nathan to "speak the truth in love" (Ephesians 4:15) to David when he
needed it?

Truth can be both freeing and frightening — even at the same time. Nathan intensified the crisis that allowed David to move to repentance. Have you ever experienced a "crisis of truth" that ultimately led you to repentance or to receiving mercy? Explain.

What do you think truth has to do with finding freedom to break the power of your shame?

JOHN 8:32. Then you will know the truth, and the truth will set you free.

Has truth ever felt like something other than freedom? If so, talk with God about that.

Jesus was a master at speaking painful — even shameful — truths into someone's life *with mercy*. Read LUKE 22:31-34 and notice how He did that.

Painful truth about Peter:

Mercy offered to Peter:

Who (if anyone) among your friends has been like a "Nathan" or like Jesus to you? Or have you already invited someone into your struggle with shame? How did he/she help you?

PRAYER PAUSE

David did it all — adultery, conspiracy, murder, cover-up, abuse of power. In his day, several of those crimes deserved the death penalty no matter how many animal sacrifices he made. So God did what David could never do for himself — He stepped in to cleanse David's heart from everything that defiled him — the sins and guilt, and all the shame too.

> *HEBREWS 9:13-14. Under the old system, the blood of goats and bulls and the ashes of a young cow could cleanse people's bodies from ceremonial impurity. Just think how much more the blood of Christ will purify our consciences from sinful deeds so that we can worship the living God. For by the power of the eternal Spirit, Christ offered himself to God as a perfect sacrifice for our sins.* (NLT)

Pause to talk with God for awhile about anything that makes you feel damaged, defiled, or dead. Claim the promise in the verse above for cleansing through Christ. And let that lead you into a time of freedom in worship. Then jot down a few notes about that experience.

Cleansing Time . . .

PAUΓE 2_DAVID FACEΓ
HEAPED-ON ΓHAME

David experienced shame because of his sin with Bathsheba and also because it was heaped on by others. King Saul tried for years to kill David. Others tried to bring him down with shaming words. But it all sent him running to God for help and mercy.

As you read David's passionate prayer below, try to find and <u>underline at least **eight** ways that people were trying to heap shame on David.</u> Also highlight any of David's emotions.

PSALMS 69:4-12

⁴ Those who hate me without cause
    outnumber the hairs on my head.
Many enemies try to destroy me with lies,
    demanding that I give back what I didn't steal.
⁵ O God, you know how foolish I am;
    my sins cannot be hidden from you.
⁶ Don't let those who trust in you be ashamed because of me,
    O Sovereign LORD of Heaven's Armies.
Don't let me cause them to be humiliated,
    O God of Israel.
⁷ For I endure insults for your sake;
    humiliation is written all over my face.
⁸ Even my own brothers pretend they don't know me;
    they treat me like a stranger.
⁹ Passion for your house has consumed me,
    and the insults of those who insult you have fallen on me.
¹⁰ When I weep and fast,
    they scoff at me.
¹¹ When I dress in burlap to show sorrow,
    they make fun of me.
¹² I am the favorite topic of town gossip,
    and all the drunks sing about me. (NLT)

We might expect David to be bitter toward God for allowing all this pain and suffering into his life. But he wasn't!

> *PSALM 69:16-18. Answer my prayers, O Lord, for your unfailing love is wonderful. Take care of me, for your mercy is so plentiful. Don't hide from your servant; answer me quickly, for I am in deep trouble! Come and redeem me; free me from my enemies.* (NLT)

From these verses, what did David do with the shame others tried to heap on him?

David frequently called out to God for *mercy.* He knew that mercy is **NOT**:

- Ignoring wrongs
- Just looking the other way
- Pretending bad things didn't really happen
- Letting scoundrels off scot-free
-
-
-

So then, what do you think mercy **IS**? Explain.

PAUSE 3_BEING A
MESSENGER OF MERCY

Coming into the light isn't a do-it-your-self project for most of us. Like David, we often need a friend like Nathan to help us face some hard truths and reconcile with God.

> *2 CORINTHIANS 5:19-20. And [God] has committed to us the message of reconciliation. We are therefore Christ's ambassadors, as though God were making his appeal through us. We implore you on Christ's behalf: Be reconciled to God.*

Who among your friends do you think might be struggling with shame? Pause a minute to consider this. It might be something traumatic like a rape or devastating divorce. But most of us deal with more ordinary things like not getting a promotion, being overweight, or living with parents because we can't afford to be on our own. Write that friend's initials here.

Do you think your friend trusts you enough to talk with you about that? Explain.

Mercy alone embraces us in our shame and moves us beyond it to a life marked by newness and restoration. The person who deeply feels his shame is able to receive the unfathomable riches of undeserved love offered to him.

— RALPH & JENNIFER ENNIS AND PAULA RINEHART,
THE ISSUE OF SHAME IN REACHING PEOPLE FOR CHRIST: WHEN GUILT-FREE ISN'T ENOUGH

To experience God's grace . . . our hearts have to be connected to it. We can certainly connect to God "vertically" through prayer, but to feel his grace completely we have to be open to the full expression of it "horizontally" through other people. To connect fully with the grace of God, we have to go to where it is, and he has chosen to put it into other people.

— DR. HENRY CLOUD AND DR. JOHN TOWNSEND, *HOW PEOPLE GROW*

Breaking the power of shame involves allowing others into our healing and transformation process, as David did. Read the following verses and underline how God can use you as His healing agents in someone else's life.

ROMANS 14:19. So let's agree to use all our energy in getting along with each other. Help others with encouraging words; don't drag them down by finding fault. (MSG)

GALATIANS 6:2. Carry each other's burdens, and in this way you will fulfill the law of Christ.

EPHESIANS 4:25. Therefore each of you must put off falsehood and speak truthfully to his neighbor, for we are all members of one body.

EPHESIANS 4:32. Be kind and compassionate to one another, forgiving each other, just as in Christ God forgave you.

From any of these verses identify one specific way a friend has met you in your shame.

Example: *My friend really listened to my struggle with the shame of my past, and he prayed for me. He carried my burden (see Galatians 6:2).*

Your Example:

From those same verses, what is one specific thing you can do to help your friend move toward freedom? Are there any tough truths you need to share with mercy?

But before others can help us, there's something important only we can do. What is that?

ROMANS 2:4. Don't you see how wonderfully kind, tolerant, and patient God is with you? Does this mean nothing to you? Can't you see that his kindness is intended to turn you from your sin? (NLT)

JAMES 5:16. Therefore confess your sins to each other and pray for each other so that you may be healed. The prayer of a righteous man is powerful and effective.

How do you believe that God desires to meet you in your place of shame and show you His kindness? Do you truly believe this?

PRAYER PAUSE

The difficulties of life and of relating to people often wound us. Some wounding is intentional, some not intentional. Nevertheless, *any* wounding that is unresolved can drive the knife of shame deeper. Healing begins when we bring our "stuff" into God's healing light as we confess to God and His safe people.

Your struggling friends may or may not be ready to hear truth from you or confess sins. But the time is always right for you to pray for them. Take a few minutes to pray for them and bring the "stuff" you know about into God's healing light. Listen for how God might want you to be a messenger of His mercy to those friends.

PAUSE 4_BREAKING THE POWER OF SHAME

VOICES OF MERCY

As you did in previous chapters, allow God's voice of tender mercy to speak to you through those in your group. Invite God to help you receive His mercy in your heart through the voices of your friends as His messengers.

PSALM 69:13-18. But I keep right on praying to you, LORD, hoping this is the time you will show _____ (person's name) favor. In your great love, O God, answer me with your sure salvation. Pull _____ out of the mire; don't let (him/her) sink! Deliver _____ from those who hate (him/her), and pull (him/her) from the deep waters. Do not let the floodwaters engulf _____, or the depths swallow (him/her), or the pit close its mouth over (him/her). Answer me, O LORD, out of the goodness of your love. Turn and take care of _____, for your mercy is so plentiful. Don't hide from _____; answer me quickly, for (he/she) is in deep trouble! Come and rescue _____; redeem (him/her) from all (his/her) foes. (NLT, personalized)

KEY THOUGHTS:

- Breaking the power of shame is a process that takes time. It's rarely a once-and-for-all event.
- Through relationships God redeems our shame as we both offer and receive mercy and truth.
- God often sends a person to deliver His truth and mercy to us.
- One way to help break the power of shame for others is to seek them out gently, inviting them to bring their struggles with shame out in the open with you, and then taking it to God together.

SUGGESTED MEMORY VERSE FOR THIS CHAPTER

FREEDOM IN TRUTH
JOHN 8:32

Then you will know the truth,
and the truth will set you free.

CHAPTER 8
TASTING GOD'S MERCY

Shame could have been Frances' middle name. "Growing up poor and black — the world just puts shame on you," her grandmother used to say. She also hated being overweight and having such crooked teeth. Her parents didn't model or teach her about personal hygiene. Kids at school targeted her with taunts and cruel jokes.

But those things were minor compared to what she suffered at home from her dad's drunken rages and his physical and sexual abuse of her. There was no protection for the kids in her home, and family "honor" kept them from seeking outside help.

Is it any wonder that she dulled her pain with apathy, sexual experimentation, alcohol and drug use? Sure, there were so many times she tried to break free from the shame of it all. But her head echoed, "If you're trash, you may as well live like trash." And so it continued . . . why risk trying to hope again?

— Adapted from *The Shame Exchange: Trading Shame for God's Mercy and Freedom* by Steve & Sally Breedlove and Ralph & Jennifer Ennis

Can you identify with Frances in any way? If so, how?

From the story and the quote below, how is shame like an echo?

What (if any) messages of shame echo in your head?

Shame is often experienced as the inner, critical voice that judges whatever we do as wrong, inferior, or worthless. Often this inner critical voice is repeating what was said to us by our parents, relatives, teachers and peers. We may have been told that we were naughty, selfish, ugly, stupid, etc. We may have been ostracized by peers at school, humiliated by teachers, treated with contempt by our parents.

— *WWW.COLUMBIAPSYCH.COM/SHAME_MILLER.HTML*

PAUSE 1_RESTORED BY JESUS

Here's a story that captures Jesus washing away the grimy stain of a woman's shame in His tender mercy. Remember that in that culture it was legally acceptable to stone someone for doing what she did. Read JOHN 8:1-11.

Where did this woman's shame come from?

   a. From her sinful behavior
   b. From the sins of others against her
   c. From her culture
   d. All of the above

What are some things you think the Pharisees themselves should have been ashamed of? What do you notice about how Jesus exposed their shame? Explain.

Sin is the mark Adam and Eve passed on to their descendants, including us. And sin has consequences. Shame, guilt, and fear of condemnation — that's the unholy triad of the human price we've all paid for sin. And the only hope to remedy all three rests on the mercy of God.

— IDENTITY: BECOMING WHO GOD SAYS I AM, CONNECT SERIES

What do you think is the difference between being *humiliated* and being *humbled*? Do you think this woman felt humiliated or humbled — or both? Explain.

How do we still "stone" people today?

Try to imagine what this woman might have written in her journal about her shame on the day before she met Jesus — and then on the day after she met Jesus. Write your thoughts here.

The Day Before...

The Day After...

How would you like to (or how have you already) experienced God's mercy in your life?

SHAME and CONDEMNATION come at us from every side — from Satan, from people, from our life circumstances, and from our own hearts. But Jesus offers mercy!

> JOHN 8:10-11. *Then Jesus stood up again and said to the woman, "Where are your accusers? Didn't even one of them condemn you?"*
> *"No, Lord," she said.*
> *And Jesus said, "Neither do I. Go and sin no more."* (NLT)

> ROMANS 8:1. *So now there is no condemnation for those who belong to Christ Jesus.* (NLT)

How does it make you feel to know that Jesus doesn't condemn you? Explain.

A NOTE FROM GOD

Imagine that you are left alone face-to-face with Jesus — with your particular guilt or shame right out in the open between you. What do you think He would say to you? Before you write that down, sit in silent listening for several minutes.

PAUSE 2_RECEIVING GOD'S LOVE

(Circle) Yes or No for each of these questions, and explain your answer.

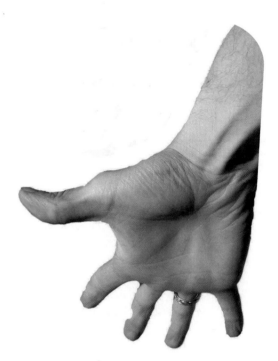

Yes   No   I usually like God.

Yes   No   I usually feel secure in God's love.

Yes   No   I usually feel worthy of God's love.

Mind   Head   I usually feel God's love with both my mind (intellect) and my heart (experience).

Many factors contribute to shame, but ultimately the problem is that we resist the reality of the Father's love. We believe, falsely, that our sin and weakness disqualify us for receiving his love.

— ANDREW COMISKEY, *STRENGTH IN WEAKNESS*

Read this beautiful expression of God's love for His people, who had been shamed and mocked by the nations around them for many years. <u>Mark</u> any phrases declaring <u>what He promises He will do for them.</u>

ZEPHANIAH 3:16-20

¹⁶On that day the announcement to Jerusalem will be, "Cheer up, Zion! Don't be afraid! For the LORD your God is living among you. He is a mighty savior. He will take delight in you with gladness. With his love, he will calm all your fears. He will rejoice over you [delights in you — NIV] with joyful songs."

¹⁸ "I will gather you who mourn for the appointed festivals; you will be disgraced no more. And I will deal severely with all who have oppressed you. I will save the weak and helpless ones; I will bring together those who were chased away. I will give glory and fame to my former exiles, wherever they have been mocked and shamed.

²⁰On that day I will gather you together and bring you home again. I will give you a good name, a name of distinction, among all the nations of the earth, as I restore your fortunes before their very eyes. I, the LORD, have spoken!" (NLT)

Do you know in your head that God, by choice, loves and delights in you? Is your heart just as sure as your head? Explain.

From all of God's "I will" promises to Israel, which one would you most want Him to promise *you*? Explain.

PAUSE 3_
UNLEARNING SHAME AND OFFERING BLESSING

Remember Frances in the opening story and the woman caught in adultery? What shaming words do you think people said to them or about them?

Can you give an example of a time you shamed somebody else with your words? Explain.

UNLEARNING THE LANGUAGE OF SHAME

The opposite of shaming someone is blessing them. Breaking the power of shame in our lives includes unlearning the language of shame — and learning the language of blessing. In these columns jot down anything you notice in these verses that will help you guard your speech or nonverbal language against shaming others.

SHAMING WORDS		LOVING WORDS
Foul *Dirty*	**EPHESIANS 4:29-32.** *Watch the way you talk. Let nothing foul or dirty come out of your mouth. Say only what helps, each word a gift.* *Don't grieve God. Don't break his heart. His Holy Spirit, moving and breathing in you, is the most intimate part of your life, making you fit for himself. Don't take such a gift for granted.* *Make a clean break with all cutting, backbiting, profane talk. Be gentle with one another, sensitive. Forgive one another as quickly and thoroughly as God in Christ forgave you.* (MSG) *COLOSSIANS 3:12-14. Since God chose you to be the holy people he loves, you must clothe yourselves with tenderhearted mercy, kindness, humility, gentleness, and patience. Make allowance for each other's faults, and forgive anyone who offends you. Remember, the Lord forgave you, so you must forgive others. Above all, clothe yourselves with love, which binds us all together in perfect harmony.* (NLT)	

If God helped you delete from your speech one hurtful word or offensive phrase that you've caught yourself saying to others (or behind their backs), what would it be? Who do you tend to use those words with? (Before answering, ask God what He would say about that.)

LEARNING THE LANGUAGE OF BLESSING

Mark whatever you notice in these passages about speaking words of blessing to others.

ROMANS 12:21. Do not be overcome by evil, but overcome evil with good.

NUMBERS 6:22-27
²² Then the LORD said to Moses, "Tell Aaron and his sons to bless the people of Israel with this special blessing:
'May the LORD bless you and protect you.
May the LORD smile on you and be gracious to you.
May the LORD show you his favor and give you his peace.'
²⁷ "Whenever Aaron and his sons bless the people of Israel in my name, I myself will bless them." (NLT)

ISAIAH 50:4. The Sovereign LORD has given me an instructed tongue, to know the word that sustains the weary.

How can we "overcome evil with good" by the words we choose?

What does God promise in verse 27 about the power of blessing others?

Remember the friend you identified in chapter 7 who may be struggling with shame? Ask God for an "instructed tongue" and a specific blessing for your friend. After you pray, write it here:

PAUSE 4_BREAKING THE POWER OF SHAME

Our struggle against shame and shaming words lasts a lifetime, because every stage of life brings different challenges. But the good news is that we can capture the mercy and blessing God provides in the struggle. From these verses, notice what Jesus is doing — and what we can do — when the voices of shame return to bother us:

> HEBREWS 12:2. Let us fix our eyes on Jesus, the author and perfecter of our faith, who for the joy set before him endured the cross, scorning its shame, and sat down at the right hand of the throne of God.

> PHILIPPIANS 4:8. Summing it all up, friends, I'd say you'll do best by filling your minds and meditating on things true, noble, reputable, authentic, compelling, gracious — the best, not the worst; the beautiful, not the ugly; things to praise, not things to curse. (MSG)

How can fixing our eyes on Jesus and filling our minds with good things put shaming accusations in their place?

Remember the echo you wrote about at the beginning of this chapter? Write it on a piece of paper — and then shred it to tiny pieces. Ask God to replace it with His blessing for you. Also write it here and be prepared to share it with your small group. Now when the echo of shame returns, look to Jesus and fill your mind with "the beautiful and not the ugly." Let God's blessing of love for you replace the old echo.

VOICES OF MERCY

Also remember this whenever you face the sting of disgrace or shame or accusation or condemnation again: Jesus is standing up for you like a bodyguard or a defense attorney. So close your group time by reading these encouraging words to one another.

ISAIAH 50:7-9

_____ (Person's name), because the Sovereign Lord helps you, you will not be disgraced.

Therefore set your face like flint, and know you will not be put to shame.

He who vindicates you, _____, is near.

Who then will bring any charges against you? Who is your accuser, _____?

Let him confront me!

It is the Sovereign LORD who helps you. Who is he that will condemn you, O _____? (NIV, personalized)

KEY THOUGHTS:

- Shaming and condemnation may come from Satan, other people, life circumstances, or our own hearts. But Jesus never condemns us. He isn't ashamed of us, either.
- God's eternal plan to break the power of our guilt and shame was for His Son Jesus to bear it all for us on the cross.
- Breaking shame's power involves learning to believe, receive, and rest secure in God's love for us and His tender mercy.
- God calls us to respond to His mercy by walking alongside others in their shame and being a voice of mercy to them.
- We can unlearn the language of shame and learn to speak the language of blessing.

SUGGESTED MEMORY VERSE FOR THIS CHAPTER

NO CONDEMNATION
ROMANS 8:1

Therefore, there is now no condemnation for those who are in Christ Jesus.

CHAPTER 9
SHAME EXCHANGED

Jason was completely stunned when his wife left him and their two small kids for another man — an elder at their church, no less! Her actions were blatant and public, played out in front of a large church and a broad community. No one seriously questioned who was at fault: she rejected counsel, support, love, and accountability from several caring friends and relatives when she bailed out on her family. Years later her children are still angry and confused from her abandonment.

Everyone told Jason it wasn't his fault. Sure, theirs wasn't a perfect marriage — but it had been a good marriage for many years. So why is it that five years later his ex-wife still doesn't feel ashamed of what she did, and is still oblivious to the pain she's caused? Jason has had a hard time going to church. He is just beginning to relate openly to old friends. What's confusing is that the person who acted shamefully feels no shame. The one who was violated still feels ashamed!

Jason's wife is the one who was unfaithful. So why do you think Jason is the one who still feels ashamed?

What do you think Jesus would say to Jason? To Jason's wife?

Can you identify with him in any way? If so, how?

PAUSE 1_GOD TASTES SHAME

Have you ever been dumped by someone you cared deeply for? In addition to hurt and anger, did you feel any shame? If so, what do you think that might have been about?

Do you think God has ever felt the sting of shame? If so, explain or give an example.

As for his chosen people of Israel, whatever shame and humiliation they endured, God also endured.

— PHILIP YANCEY, *DISAPPOINTMENT WITH GOD*

As a matter of fact, God compares Himself to a rejected parent and a dumped husband who has been humiliated and disgraced. Here's one place in the Bible where He expresses how much this hurts Him. He's using an allegory to describe the nation of Israel's on-again, off-again response to His loving pursuit of them. As you read each paragraph, try to express one or two specific emotions that God might have been experiencing, such as sympathy, tenderness, or frustration.

¹ Then another message came to me from the LORD: "Son of man, confront Jerusalem with her detestable sins. Give her this message from the Sovereign LORD: You are nothing but a Canaanite! Your father was an Amorite and your mother a Hittite. On the day you were born, no one cared about you. Your umbilical cord was not cut, and you were never washed, rubbed with salt, and wrapped in cloth. No one had the slightest interest in you; no one pitied you or cared for you. On the day you were born, you were unwanted, dumped in a field and left to die.

⁶ "But I came by and saw you there, helplessly kicking about in your own blood. As you lay there, I said, 'Live!' And I helped you to thrive like a plant in the field. You grew up and became a beautiful jewel. Your breasts became full, and your body hair grew, but you were still naked. And when I passed by again, I saw that you were old enough for love. So I wrapped my cloak around you to cover your nakedness and declared my marriage vows. I made a covenant with you, says the Sovereign LORD, and you became mine.

⁹ "Then I bathed you and washed off your blood, and I rubbed fragrant oils into your skin. I gave you expensive clothing of fine linen and silk, beautifully embroidered, and sandals made of fine goatskin leather. I gave you lovely jewelry, brace-lets, beautiful necklaces, a ring for your nose, ear-rings for your ears, and a lovely crown for your head. And so you were adorned with gold and silver. Your clothes were made of fine linen and were beautifully embroidered. You ate the finest foods — choice flour, honey, and olive oil — and became more beautiful than ever. You looked like a queen, and so you were! Your fame soon spread throughout the world because of your beauty. I dressed you in my splendor and perfected your beauty, says the Sovereign LORD. (NLT)

Describe several ways God took loving initiatives toward the "abandoned child" Israel.

Now describe how Israel responded to God, and how God felt about that.

EZEKIEL 16:15-16

GOD'S EMOTIONS

But you thought your fame and beauty were your own. So you gave yourself as a prostitute to every man who came along. Your beauty was theirs for the asking. You used the lovely things I gave you to make shrines for idols, where you played the prostitute. Unbelievable! How could such a thing ever happen? (NLT)

"I'll tell you how I feel! I feel like a rejected parent. I find a baby girl lying in a ditch, near death. I take her home and make her my daughter. I clean her, pay for her schooling, feed her. I dote on her, clothe her, hang jewelry on her. Then one day she runs away. I hear reports of her debased life. When my name comes up, she curses me.

"I'll tell you how I feel! I feel like a jilted lover. I found my lover thin and wasted, abused, but I brought her home and made her beauty shine. She is my precious one, the most beautiful woman in the world to me, and I lavish on her gifts and love. And yet she forsakes me. She pants after my best friends, my enemies — anyone. She stands by a highway and under every spreading tree and, worse than a prostitute, she pays people to have sex with her. I feel betrayed, abandoned, cuckolded."

— PHILIP YANCEY, *DISAPPOINTMENT WITH GOD*

But the story doesn't end with shame and disgrace! Read EZEKIEL 39:25-29. What does God promise to do so that the memory of their shame will fade away?

JE/U/ AL/O FACED /HAME

On the cross God in Christ endured the ultimate humiliation. For our weaknesses and shame, God allowed himself to become weak and full of shame. God was strung up naked before a mocking, jeering public. He subjected himself to the worst kind of exposure in order to make a way for us, his creation, who have been subject to the exposure of sin and shame ourselves.

— ANDREW COMISKEY, *STRENGTH IN WEAKNESS*

Consider this description of Jesus at the most shameful point in His entire life: being humiliated and executed publicly as a convicted criminal.

HEBREWS 12:2. Let us fix our eyes on Jesus, the author and perfecter of our faith, who for the joy set before him endured the cross, scorning its shame [or "despising the shame" — NASB], and sat down at the right hand of the throne of God.

Why do you think Jesus was willing to die a shameful death on the cross? What do you think He was feeling, thinking, or telling Himself that helped Him endure the pain and shame of the cross? (Consider what — or who — was "the joy set before Him.")

de-spise: *to regard with contempt or scorn; to dislike intensely; loathe; to regard as unworthy of one's interest or concern.*

— HOUGHTON MIFFLIN AMERICAN HERITAGE DICTIONARY OF THE ENGLISH LANGUAGE
HTTP://EDUCATION.YAHOO.COM/REFERENCE/DICTIONARY/

What do you think it might mean for us to follow Jesus' example by "despising" or "scorning" the shame in our lives?

Do you believe Jesus can relate to you in your shame? If so, explain why from reading HEBREWS 4:15 in your Bible.

The cross of Jesus is not just about forensic guilt and an impossible debt. It is also about identity-level shame that is exposed for the world to see and to mock. Jesus was jeered by the masses in Jerusalem. He was ridiculed by the Pharisees, mocked as a helpless liar. He was crucified, naked and exposed — an unimaginable shame for a Jewish man. A laughingstock, He was spat upon, abused and victimized — think of what this felt like! All of the shameful treatment and exposure you might feel in your soul was heaped on Him in one outpouring of vitriolic hate. It is not just about what happened to Jesus; it is about what happened in Him. The anchor of His soul had always been His Father's love and care, but on the cross, He experienced abandonment and rejection.

— STEVE & SALLY BREEDLOVE AND RALPH & JENNIFER ENNIS,
THE SHAME EXCHANGE: TRADING SHAME FOR GOD'S MERCY AND FREEDOM

PAUSE 2_GOD'S SOLUTION FOR OUR SHAME

Read this powerful passage about God's eternal plan for breaking the power of our guilt and shame. As you read, mark key ideas.

ISAIAH 53:2-10
2-6The servant grew up before God — a scrawny seedling,
*   a scrubby plant in a parched field.*
There was nothing attractive about him,
*   nothing to cause us to take a second look.*
He was looked down on and passed over,
*   a man who suffered, who knew pain firsthand.*
One look at him and people turned away.
*   We looked down on him, thought he was scum.*
But the fact is, it was our pains he carried —
*   our disfigurements, all the things wrong with us.*
We thought he brought it on himself,
*   that God was punishing him for his own failures.*
But it was our sins that did that to him
*   that ripped and tore and crushed him — our sins!*
He took the punishment, and that made us whole.
*   Through his bruises we get healed.*
We're all like sheep who've wandered off and gotten lost.
*   We've all done our own thing, gone our own way.*
And GOD has piled all our sins, everything we've done wrong, on him, on him.

7-9 He was beaten, he was tortured,
*   but he didn't say a word. . . .*
He died without a thought for his own welfare,
*   beaten bloody for the sins of my people. . . .*

10Still, it's what GOD had in mind all along,
*   to crush him with pain.*
The plan was that he give himself as an offering for sin
*   so that he'd see life come from it — life, life, and more life.*
*   And GOD's plan will deeply prosper through him.* (MSG)

If someone asked you to explain what God's solution is for our guilt and shame, what would you say?

How does this give you hope?

After everything you've studied and experienced in this Bible study, where is your heart right now in terms of trusting Jesus — really trusting Him? Explain.

PAUSE 3_JESUS CARRIES OUR SHAME

Consider what Christ's sacrifice and shed blood have to do with our freedom.

> *HEBREWS 9:14. Think how much more the blood of Christ cleans up our whole lives, inside and out. Through the Spirit, Christ offered himself as an unblemished sacrifice, freeing us from all those dead-end efforts to make ourselves respectable, so that we can live all out for God.* (MSG)

From this verse, what can God's mercy, through Christ, free us *from*?

What can God's mercy, through Christ, free us *for* or free us *to do or experience*?

As strange as it sounds, Jesus became sin for us on the cross (see 2 Corinthians 5:20-21). Why? Jesus exchanged all that He was for all that we are — our sin, our guilt, our debt, our curse, and our shame. This is not just some spiritual hocus-pocus. He actually bore it all and became it all. He took and became all the shame you feel and all the shame you bear so you wouldn't have to bear it, or be it, anymore.

— STEVE & SALLY BREEDLOVE AND RALPH & JENNIFER ENNIS,
THE SHAME EXCHANGE: TRADING SHAME FOR GOD'S MERCY AND FREEDOM

From the following verses, summarize in your own words how God and Jesus feel about us.

> HEBREWS 2:11. *Both the one who makes men holy and those who are made holy are of the same family. So Jesus is not ashamed to call them brothers.*

> HEBREWS 4:15-16. *For we do not have a high priest who is unable to sympathize with our weaknesses, but we have one who has been tempted in every way, just as we are — yet was without sin. Let us then approach the throne of grace with confidence, so that we may receive mercy and find grace to help us in our time of need.*

How does it impact your heart to know that Jesus experienced the shaming power of others and is also in touch with the reality of your shame?

Some of us have family members we are faintly or deeply ashamed of. . . . But the Son of Man, Jesus Himself, holds us up before all creation as his brothers. We do not embarrass Him.

— SALLY BREEDLOVE, *CHOOSING REST*

If you were Jason's friend (from the opening story), what would you say to him now?

Imagine how David felt when he wrote these words about a very humiliating time in his life. Then imagine God's gentle hands lifting up his head, to gaze into his eyes with love.

> PSALM 3:1-3
> O LORD, I have so many enemies;
>   so many are against me.
> So many are saying,
>   "God will never rescue him!"
>
> But you, O LORD, are a shield around me,
>   you are my glory, the one who holds my head high. (NLT)

PRAYER PAUSE

Quiet your heart and mind for several minutes. Imagine yourself walking right up to Jesus to get what He is so ready to give you (Hebrews 4:16). Also imagine God the Father tenderly putting His hand under your chin and lifting your head to meet His compassionate gaze. How does your heart respond to God Himself inviting you to come close to Him, lifting your head and shielding you from the power of your shame?

Journal or draw . . .

PAUSE 4_BREAKING THE POWER OF SHAME

VOICES OF MERCY

Let God use your voices to express His mercy to one another. Looking into each other's eyes, speak these words, filling in the blanks with the person's name.

HEBREWS 4:15-16; 2:11

For you do not have a high priest who is unable to sympathize with [your] weaknesses, _____, but you have one who has been tempted in every way, just as we all are — yet was without sin.

Both the one who makes men holy and we who are made holy are of the same family. So Jesus is not ashamed to call [you] _____ His brother / sister.

So, _____, approach the throne of grace with confidence, so that you may receive mercy and find grace to help you in your time of need. (NIV, personalized)

Therefore God is not ashamed to be called your God, _____ (person's name).

KEY THOUGHTS:

- God can intimately relate to my shame. Jesus also experienced others trying to put Him to shame.
- In His crucifixion and death, Jesus took my shame upon Him and tasted its pain and humiliation.
- Neither God nor Jesus is ashamed of me, and Jesus protects me in the presence of my accusers by declaring me "family."

SUGGESTED MEMORY VERSE
FOR THIS CHAPTER

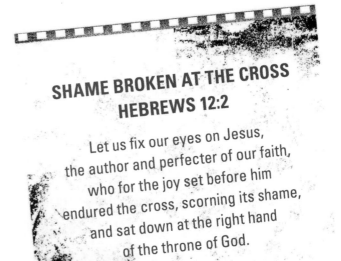

SHAME BROKEN AT THE CROSS
HEBREWS 12:2

Let us fix our eyes on Jesus,
the author and perfecter of our faith,
who for the joy set before him
endured the cross, scorning its shame,
and sat down at the right hand
of the throne of God.

CHAPTER 10
CELEBRATING YOUR GROUP

As you and your group have gone through this Bible study together, your relationships have deepened. You've learned much from each other — truths, joys, pains. So now we encourage you to plan a celebration. Prepare by jotting down some responses to the questions in Pauses 1 and 2 ahead of time. When you get together, take some time to discuss the questions in Pause 3 by reflecting back, envisioning forward, and pausing to affirm and pray for one another.

PAUƧE 1_FACING ƧHAME AND FINDING MERCY

Reread this quote from chapter 1, marking whatever touches you:

> We may trust God with our past as heartily as with our future. It will not hurt so long as we do not try to hide things, so long as we are ready to bow our heads in hearty shame where it is fit that we should be ashamed. For to be ashamed is a holy and blessed thing.
>
> Shame is a thing to shame only those who want to appear, not those who want to be. Shame is to shame those who want to pass their examination, not those who want to get into the heart of things.... To be humbly ashamed is to be plunged in the cleansing bath of truth.
>
> — *FROM* AN ANTHOLOGY OF GEORGE MACDONALD, *EDITED BY C. S. LEWIS*

FACING ƧHAME

What types of shame have you identified in your own life — past or current?

What have you discovered about heaped-on shame versus healthy, deserved shame that comes with being human and a sinner?

What have you learned about hiding and the healing process of opening up your shame to others?

FINDING MERCY

How have Jesus and others met you in your experience of shame?

As you reflect on your study, what do you still need to trust God with about your past?

About your future?

As God's mercy frees us from the bonds of shame, He also frees us for deeper intimacy with Him. How has your intimacy with God grown as you have been drawn deeper into His heart through this study?

PAUSE 2_EXCHANGING OUR SHAME

As you read the following quote, imagine the scene and think about the exchange Jesus offers at the cross:

At some point it became clear to Jesus that the Father's will included the most shameful experiences a man can face — total exposure, full rejection, complete abandonment, helplessness, mockery, and accusation. His closest companions misunderstood Him. The crowd believed the worst about Him. He was silent before the heaped-on shame. His hands hung limply at His side, unable to wipe away the spit trickling into His eyes. They jerked at His beard until it was ragged and bloody. Everyone saw His friends desert Him. His clothes were stripped away as His body was nailed to the cross. He lost the ability to control bodily functions. And finally the Father turned His back on Him as He bore the sin of all humanity. . . .

Shame. Jesus Christ embraced it. It was the Father's plan. Why? The answer is remarkably simple: He wanted sons and daughters, a family to love and be loved by. Just as we need His righteousness in exchange for our guilt, we must have our shame exchanged for His Sonship, our ashes for His beauty, our weakness for His strength. Take a moment to slowly go through the questions below and allow God to whisper in your ear as you sift through the ashes of your shame.

— STEVE & SALLY BREEDLOVE AND RALPH & JENNIFER ENNIS,
THE SHAME EXCHANGE: TRADING SHAME FOR GOD'S MERCY AND FREEDOM

Through this study we've discovered that some shame is true shame; it is the identity shame we bear as humans and as sinful beings. We identified various ways we tend to cover it up, deny it, get rid of it, or become numb to it. And yet the reality of our true shame remains. Could it be that God actually uses our shame to draw us to Himself? Could the shame we feel about our condition (not the shame others heap upon us) actually be a gift? For in embracing our true shame Jesus offers an extravagant exchange:

"Jesus exchanged all that He was for all that we are — our sin, our guilt, our debt, our curse and our shame."
—STEVE & SALLY BREEDLOVE AND RALPH & JENNIFER ENNIS,
THE SHAME EXCHANGE: TRADING SHAME FOR GOD'S MERCY AND FREEDOM

He invites us to trade our sin, shame, and guilt for His mercy, forgiveness, and healing presence.

What specifically do you need to face and lay down at Jesus feet? Write a prayer to Jesus that does this:

What do you want and need to receive from Jesus in exchange?

YOUR RESPONSE

Some of you may have never accepted the invitation to become His son or daughter. As part of the exchange at the cross, Jesus, your brother, offers you the gift of adoption into the family of God. God's unchanging plan has always been to adopt you into His family through Jesus Christ (see EPHESIANS 1:6-7). And it gives Him great pleasure each time someone comes to Him. When you respond to God's invitation to become His child, He promises to make you new from the inside out (see 2 CORINTHIANS 5:17).

A MOMENT WITH GOD

God is inviting you to become His child and to exchange your shame and ashes for His acceptance and beauty (ISAIAH 61:3).

Talk with Him awhile about your response.

PAUƧE 3_CELEBRATING YOUR GROUP

Take some time together to discuss these summary questions:

REFLECT BACK

- Share how you have benefited from this group of fellow spiritual journeyers.
- How has your walk with God been impacted?
- How has your daily lifestyle changed?
- What emotions surface as you reflect back on your times together?

Somewhere deep down, we know that if we are to survive we must come together and rediscover ways to connect with each other, and with the earth that supports our collective life. We are social beings who need one another not just for physical survival but also for spiritual sustenance as we journey together. So our individuality only makes sense in the context of community, where we are free to become ourselves.

— JONATHAN S. CAMPBELL WITH JENNIFER CAMPBELL,
THE WAY OF JESUS: A JOURNEY OF FREEDOM FOR PILGRIMS AND WANDERERS

ENVIƧION FORWARD

- What are your spiritual needs as you consider the next phase of your journey?
- In what environment might these needs be met?
- What continuing relationships will you have with the people in this group (casual friendship to in-depth involvement)?
- Which other people do you know who could benefit from studying this topic or another book in the Connect series?
- Should one or more people from this group team up to facilitate a new group? Is God leading anyone to be a part of a new group?

PAUSE TO AFFIRM

- Do you want to express a thank you or affirmation to anyone in the group who has impacted your life?
- Take time to do that. Pause to pray . . . Spend time together praying.
- Thank God for this part of your journey. Praise Him for Who He is. Don't hurry through this time.

PAUSE 4_BREAKING THE POWER OF SHAME

Close your time together by reading the following verses out loud in unison to one another. Or go around the circle and have each person read one verse aloud. Perhaps these words will comfort you as they did when Isaiah spoke them, comforting the people of Israel with God's promise of a coming Savior who would exchange their shame for joy. This passage has been personalized by inserting the words "you" and "your" occasionally.

ISAIAH 61:1-7
¹ The Spirit of GOD, the Master, is on me
    because GOD anointed me.
    He sent me to preach good news to you poor,
    heal you heartbroken,
Announce freedom to all you captives,
    pardon all you prisoners.
² GOD sent me to announce the year of his grace to you —
    a celebration of God's destruction of your enemies —
    and to comfort all you who mourn,
³ To care for the needs of all you who mourn in Zion,
    give you bouquets of roses instead of ashes,
Messages of joy instead of news of doom,
    a praising heart instead of a languid spirit.
Rename you "Oaks of Righteousness"
    planted by GOD to display his glory.
⁴ You'll rebuild the old ruins,
    raise a new city out of the wreckage.
You'll start over on the ruined cities,
    take the rubble left behind and make it new. . . .
⁷ Instead of your shame,
    you will receive a double portion,
And instead of disgrace
    you will rejoice in your inheritance;
Your inheritance in the land will be doubled
    and your joy go on forever.
(MSG and NIV personalized)

THE SHAME EXCHANGE
ISAIAH 61:3

To all who mourn in Israel,
he will give a crown of beauty for ashes,
a joyous blessing instead of mourning,
festive praise instead of despair.
In their righteousness, they will be like great oaks
that the LORD has planted
for his own glory. (NLT)

WHY MEMORIZE SCRIPTURE?

You won't find the word "memorize" in the Bible, but the concept is there both in command and in example. We are encouraged to:

- "treasure, store up, hide, study, reflect on, delight in, and not forget" God's words. (Psalm 119:9-16; 37:31)
- "lay hold of . . . pay attention . . . listen closely." (Proverbs 4:4,20-22)
- "wear [my commands] like a necklace . . . write them deep within your heart." (Proverbs 3:3)
- "Always treasure my commands. Guard my teachings as your most precious possession. Tie them on your fingers as a reminder . . . write them on the tablet of your heart." (Proverbs 7:1-3)
- "it is good to keep these sayings deep within yourself . . . ready on your lips." (Proverbs 22:18)
- "meditate on [God's words] day and night." (Joshua 1:8)
- "talk about [God's commandments] when you sit at home . . . walk along the road . . . lie down and when you get up" especially with your children. (Deuteronomy 6:7-8)

These verses and others also explain the reasons for and benefits of memorizing Scripture:

- "that I might not sin against you . . . [my] feet do not slip." (Psalm 119:9-16; 37:31)
- "they bring life and radiant health." (Proverbs 4:22)
- "find favor with both God and people . . . have a good reputation." (Proverbs 3:4)
- "you may be sure to obey all that is written in it. Only then will you succeed." (Joshua 1:8)
- So that you will "have all of them ready on your lips." (Proverbs 22:18)
- "Your words . . . sustain me . . . bring me great joy and are my heart's delight." (Jeremiah 15:16)
- To "impress them on your children." (Deuteronomy 6:7)

Perhaps even more compelling than these reasons is seeing how powerfully God can use a person who has taken the time and effort to consistently memorize Scripture. When Jesus faced Satan (see Matthew 4:4-11), He drew from the many verses of Scripture that He had memorized in His youth to pinpoint Satan's deception and resist temptation. When Peter addressed the huge crowd on the day of Pentecost, he was given no time to consult his concordance and prepare a message! Because he had made Scripture memory a priority in his life, he could quote from three different Old Testament passages that helped bring 3,000 people to the Lord. If you long to equip yourself to counteract Satan, resist sin, trust and obey God, listen to God's voice, and minister to others, there is *no better investment of your time than memorizing Scripture.*

PRACTICAL TIPS FOR MEMORIZING SCRIPTURE

Here are some good, practical suggestions for memorizing:

- Memorize one phrase at a time.
- Copy each verse onto a little card.
- Carry the verse cards around with you.
- Put them on your computer.
- Review them out loud. Often.
- Write them out until you can do so accurately.
- Meditate on them.
- Pray over them.
- Tell a friend what they mean to you.
- Put yourself to sleep at night thinking about them.

And look forward to listening to God speak to you from these verses for the rest of your life!

SCRIPTURE MEMORY VERSES

SHAME REDEEMED

GENESIS 50:20

You intended to harm me, but God intended it for good to accomplish what is now being done, the saving of many lives.

BRINGING SHAME TO LIGHT

1 JOHN 1:9

If we confess our sins, he is faithful and just and will forgive us our sins and purify us from all unrighteousness.

GOD'S DELIGHT

ZEPHANIAH 3:17

The LORD your God is with you, he is mighty to save. He will take great delight in you, he will quiet you with his love, he will rejoice over you with singing.

FREEDOM IN TRUTH

JOHN 8:32

Then you will know the truth, and the truth will set you free.

SHAME BROKEN AT THE CROSS

HEBREWS 12:2

Let us fix our eyes on Jesus, the author and perfecter of our faith, who for the joy set before him endured the cross, scorning its shame, and sat down at the right hand of the throne of God.

REST FROM SELF-CONDEMNATION

1 JOHN 3:19-20 (NIV, PERSONALIZED)

This then is how you can know that you belong to the truth, and how you can set your heart at rest in his presence whenever your heart condemns you. For God is greater than your heart, and he knows everything.

SHAME FORGOTTEN

ISAIAH 54:4-5

Do not be afraid; you will not suffer shame. Do not fear disgrace; you will not be humiliated. You will forget the shame of your youth and remember no more the reproach of your widowhood. For . . . the Holy One of Israel is your Redeemer; he is called the God of all the earth.

WORKING FOR GOOD

ROMANS 8:28

And we know that in all things God works for the good of those who love him, who have been called according to his purpose.

NO CONDEMNATION

ROMANS 8:1

Therefore, there is now no condemnation for those who are in Christ Jesus.

THE SHAME EXCHANGE

ISAIAH 61:3

To all who mourn in Israel, he will give a crown of beauty for ashes, a joyous blessing instead of mourning, festive praise instead of despair. In their righteousness, they will be like great oaks that the Lord has planted for his own glory. (NLT)

FURTHER READING

Breedlove, S. & S., and Ennis, R. & J. *The Shame Exchange: Trading Shame for God's Mercy and Freedom.* Colorado Springs, CO: NavPress, 2009.

Cloud, H. and Townsend, J. *How People Grow: What the Bible Reveals About Personal Growth.* Grand Rapids, MI: Zondervan, 2001.

Comiskey, A. *Strength in Weakness.* Downers Grove, IL: InterVarsity, 2003.

Ennis, R. & J., and Rinehart, P. *The Issue of Shame in Reaching People for Christ: When Guilt-Free Isn't Enough.* Colorado Springs, CO: NavPress, 2004.

Frost, J. *Experiencing Father's Embrace.* Shippensburg, PA: Destiny Image, 2006.

Humbert, C. *Deceived by Shame, Desired by God.* Colorado Springs, CO: NavPress, 2001.

Manning, B. *A Stranger to Self-Hatred: A Glimpse of Jesus,* Denville, NJ: Dimension Books, 1982.

Neal, C. *Dancing in the Arms of God: Finding Intimacy and Fulfillment by Following His Lead,* Grand Rapids, MI: Zondervan, 1995.

Rinehart, P. *Sex and the Soul of a Woman.* Grand Rapids, MI: Zondervan, 2004.

Senter, R. *Longing for Love: Conversations with a Compassionate Heavenly Father.* Colorado Springs, CO: NavPress, 1991.

Smedes, L. *Shame and Grace: Healing the Shame We Don't Deserve.* New York, NY: Harpers Collins Publishers, Reprint 1994.

Thrall, B., McNicol, B., and Lynch, J. *TrueFaced, TrueFaced Experience Guide.* Colorado Springs, CO: NavPress, 2003.

Townsend, J. *Hiding from Love: How to Change the Withdrawal Patterns that Isolate and Imprison You.* Grand Rapids, MI: Zondervan, 1991.

Wilson, S. *Released from Shame.* Downer's Grove, IL: InterVarsity, Revised edition, 2002.

Wright, A. *Shame Off You: Overcoming the Tyrant Within.* Sisters, OR: Multnomah, 2005.

APPENDIX A
BIBLICAL USE OF "SHAME"

The English word "shame" and its different forms appear about 190 times in the Old Testament and 46 times in the New Testament. These occurrences are translations of at least ten different Hebrew and seven different Greek roots and many more Hebrew and Greek words.

Two primary meanings of "shame" appear in Scripture, some describing various states of mind and others describing a physical state. The states of mind may be classified into three broad categories: (1) those where an individual is or might be the object of contempt, derision, or humiliation; (2) those where he feels bashful or shy; (3) those where he feels respect or awe. The physical states involve a degree of exposure or nudity, or the words are used as euphemisms for the sexual organs.

The most frequent usage by far involves the ideas connected with contempt, derision, and humiliation. Shame follows when the law of God is disregarded or forgotten (Hosea 4:6-7). God sends shame upon the enemies of his people (Psalm 132:18). It is the result of sin and is removed in the day of liberty and restoration (Isaiah 61:7). It appears at times to be a punishment (Psalm 44:7,9,15). In contrast, it is also sometimes a positive preventive expression of the grace of God (Ezekiel 43:10). It may induce positive action (Judges 3:25). False shame refers to something that is actually not shameful, such as our allegiance to Christ, and should be avoided (Mark 8:38). There is also a figurative use of the term, as in Isaiah 24:23 and in Jude 13.

Shame referring to being shy or bashful only occurs a few times. A clear example is the statement concerning the man and his wife before the fall in Genesis 2:25. The usage, which represents awe or respect is also rare. An Old Testament instance is Ezra 9:6; and there is the apostolic injunction of 1 Timothy 2:9. In the former instance, the common Hebrew root *bôš*, which appears on over ninety other occasions in the Old Testament text in the *Qal* stem alone, is used; whereas 1 Timothy 2:9 is the only passage where *aids* occurs in the New Testament.

The uses of the words with a physical reference are concerned with nakedness. These occurrences are not frequent.

The biblical concept of shame is basically that of the mental state of humiliation due to sin and to departure from the law of God, which brings disgrace and rejection by both God and man. The development of the concept is most extensive in the prophets and in the Pauline epistles. The references to matters connected with sex are illustrative or figurative and do not indicate that there is any more basic connection between shame and sexual functions than between shame and other functions that may occasion embarrassment by sinful use.

BIBLIOGRAPHY.

Kittell, Gerhard. Friedrich, Gerhard. Bromiley, Geoffrey W. *Theological Dictionary of the New Testament*. Grand Rapids, MI: Wm. B. Eerdmans Publishing, 1974, 189-191.

Brown, Colin. *The New International Dictionary of New Testament Theology*. Grand Rapids, MI: Zondervan, 1986, 561-564.

Marshall, I. Howard. Packer, J.I. Wiseman, D.J. Millard, A.R. *New Bible Dictionary, Third Edition*. Downers Grove, IL: InterVarsity, 1996.

CONNECT SERIES OVERVIEW

CONNECT is designed to help you discover and embrace the truth Jesus spoke of in a holistic way. We long to see you enjoying life as a member of God's kingdom and family, deeply experiencing His presence, knowing His truth, resting in His love, and confident in His hope. These studies are designed to be used in small groups where people can encourage, trust, and support each other on their spiritual journeys.

CONNECT is a series of personal and group study books. These studies will present foundational biblical principles for primary relationships in life. Jesus summed up what life is all about when He said,

> "Love the Lord your God with all your heart and with all your soul and with all your mind." This is the first and greatest commandment. And the second is like it: "Love your neighbor as yourself" (Matthew 22:37-39).

Growing in your love for God, for others, and for yourself while managing your personal life in ways that honor Him — now that is a real spiritual journey!

In case this is your first experience in the CONNECT series — or even if you have journeyed through other studies before you picked up this one — this overview may help you connect some dots.

GOD: Connecting with His Outrageous Love is about receiving God's love and loving Him in response.

IDENTITY: Becoming Who God Says I Am and **SOUL: Embracing My Sexuality and Emotions** are about discovering who God says we are and learning to live out of that true identity.

RELATIONSHIPS: Bringing Jesus into My World is about loving people — all kinds of people. Because if we're loving God and ourselves, then loving people will happen naturally.

LIFE: Thriving in a Complex World is about living life well with Jesus.

FREEDOM: Breaking the Power of Shame invites you to face shame, whatever its source, and experience God's mercy, healing, and freedom.

Our prayer is that we all will grow in deeper intimacy with God from a heart of worship as we humbly follow Jesus' ways, truth, and life!

ABOUT THE AUTHORS

RALPH ENNIS is the Director of Intercultural Training and Development for The Navigators. Ralph and his wife, Jennifer, have ministered with The Navigators since 1975 in a variety of areas, including at Norfolk military bases, Princeton University, Richmond Community, Glen Eyrie Leadership Development Institute, and with The CoMission in Moscow, Russia. Ralph has a master's degree in Intercultural Relations. Some of his publications include *Searching the Ordinary for Meaning; Breakthru: Discover Your Spiritual Gifts and Primary Roles; Successfit: Decision Making Preferences; An Introduction to the Russian Soul;* and *The Issue of Shame in Reaching People for Christ.*

Ralph and Jennifer currently live in Raleigh, North Carolina. They have four married children and eleven grandchildren.

JUDY GOMOLL is Director of Resource Development for The Navigators National Training Team. Before joining The Navigators, Judy was an educator with a specialty in curriculum development. Judy and her husband, George, served with The Navigators as missionaries in Uganda and Kenya for fifteen years, where they helped pioneer ministries in communities, churches, and at Makerere University. Judy led in leader training and designing of contextualized discipleship materials and methods.

Judy has two master's degrees — one in Curriculum and Instruction and another in Organizational Leadership. She and George live in Parker, Colorado.

DENNIS STOKES has been serving with The Navigators since 1973. During that time he has ministered on collegiate staff, as well as being a collegiate trainer and national training consultant. Dennis has designed, developed, and led seven summer training programs for The Navigators and was the training coordinator for The CoMission project to the former Soviet Union. He is ordained and speaks at training events, conferences, and in church pulpits in the U.S. and twelve different countries. He also leads and participates on numerous training teams. In his role as the National Training Director for the U.S. Navigators, Dennis leads out in strategic planning, leading, and implementing national initiatives for staff training and development.

Dennis and his wife, Ellen, live in Erie, Colorado, and have three children — Christopher, Cheryl, and Amy.

CHRISTINE WEDDLE is Associate Director of National Training and Staff Development and has been on staff with The Navigators since 1997. She first connected with The Navigators when she joined The CoMission Training Team. In this role she assisted in the planning and organization of staff training events in the U.S., Russia, and the Ukraine.

Since moving to Colorado Springs in 1998, she has directed numerous national training and staff development events. She specializes in developing adult learning environments and visual resources.

REBECCA GOLDSTONE is a National Training Team consultant for The Navigators. Before joining The Navigators, Rebecca was a consulting partner with The Navigators in training and development for The CoMission project staff and leaders from the former Soviet countries. After leaving The CoMission, Rebecca pioneered and developed a cross-cultural urban ministry in Santa Ana, California. She is a training consultant, life coach, and serves on the faculty of Hope International University. Her role on the National Training Team consists of creating and editing resources related to spiritual transformation and strategic tools to equip leaders ministering to the millennial generation.

Rebecca and her husband, Marc, live in Irvine, California and have two children.

Connect Even More!

The CONNECT series is designed to help you discover and embrace the truth Jesus spoke of in a holistic way. By using the series in a small group, you will find encouragement, trust, and support from others as you travel together on this spiritual journey.

God: Connecting with His Outrageous Love
Ralph Ennis, Judy Gomoll, Dennis Stokes, Christine Weddle
978-1-60006-258-2

This study presents a foundational biblical principle for primary relationships in life: receiving God's love and loving Him in response.

Identity: Becoming Who God Says I Am
Ralph Ennis, Judy Gomoll, Dennis Stokes, Christine Weddle
978-1-60006-259-9

Discover who God says you are and learn to live out your true identity by loving God, others, and yourself.

Soul: Embracing My Sexuality and Emotions
Ralph Ennis, Judy Gomoll, Rebecca Goldstone, Dennis Stokes, Christine Weddle
978-1-60006-262-9

Find out how growing in your love for God, for others, and for yourself will help manage your personal life in ways that honor Him.

Relationships: Bringing Jesus into My World
Ralph Ennis, Judy Gomoll, Rebecca Goldstone, Dennis Stokes, Christine Weddle
9-781-60006-261-2

Receiving God's love and in turn loving others is God's plan for us. But loving others as ourselves is not always easy. Learn how to reach out in love to family, friends, and others who may be more difficult to love.

Life: Thriving in a Complex World
Ralph Ennis, Judy Gornoll, Dennis Stokes, Christine Weddle
978-1-60006-260-5

Study five unfolds all the CONNECT themes of living life well with Jesus. Study them in order or individually, but be ready to connect in a powerful way that will change your life.

To order copies, call NavPress at 1-800-366-7788, or log on to www.navpress.com.

NAVPRESS